The History Of Your Bible

proving the King James to be the perfectly preserved words of God.

Terence D. McLean

Copyright © 2007
All rights reserved. No part of this book may be reproduced or transmitted in any form or by any means, electronic or mechanical, digital or analog, including photocopying, or placement in any information storage or retrieval system, multi-media, or internet system, without express written permission from the publisher.

Scripture quotations in this book are from
the King James Bible,
God's perfectly preserved words.

Discerning The Times Publishing Co., Inc.
Post Office Box 87
Alpha OH 45301-0087

International Standard Book Number
ISBN-13: 978-0-9789863-3-9
ISBN-10: 0-9789863-3-4

Where to find...

Setting forth the premise 5
5600 manuscripts, no originals 10
Most frequently attacked verses 13
Inspiration, utilization, preservation 19
Adamantius Origen 28
Emperor Constantine 30
English translations before 1611 44
Bancroft's charge to the translators 47
Five "revisions" of the King James 48
Orthography, Calligraphy 49
King James Bible statistics 53
Westcott-Hort belief system 54
Truth found only in the King James 59
Testimonies of believers and infidels 64
Missing verses chart 72
Omissions of names of deity chart 73
Bodmer, Beatty papyrus 75
Afterward Article 82
Bibliography 86

Myles Coverdale Bible, 1535, cover page.

It was Coverdale who said: "It shall greatly help ye to understand Scripture if thou mark not only what is spoken or wrythen, but of whom, with what words, at what time, where, to what intent, with what circumstances, considering what goeth before and what followeth after."

The History Of Your Bible

Before we get started, allow me to remind you that each of us employs three vocabularies: spoken, written and reading.

Our conversational vocabulary uses the fewest and the shortest words and our spoken grammar is often flawed. When we write, we do better. We use more of the words we know and we tend to arrange them better than when we speak.

When we read, we expand our vocabulary's horizon, we learn new words, and we tend to notice both grammatical errors and grammatical correctness that escape us while writing or speaking.

For that reason, what you are about to read is far superior to this same message as it was heard in more than one hundred fifty churches. Radio broadcasts of this message are not as well done, precise or complete as what you are about to read, and the more than twenty thousand audio tapes of this message distributed world-wide are inferior to what you are now reading.

While you and I can understand and agree with the concept that we employ three vocabularies, God has but one and His would be perfect. Using human instrumentation, by inspiration, God delivered His perfect words over a period of more than fourteen hundred years.

What we will study is where we can locate God's perfect words today and how the Lord got them to us more than twenty centuries after they were inspired.

What we will study is fact-packed, fast paced and intense. And perhaps even shocking.

We will see that we need not rely on Greek, Hebrew or Aramaic language studies, nor need we covet the original manuscripts which simply do not exist. All I would ask, as you read on, is that you be neither prejudiced against me nor prejudiced for me. Let the facts speak for themselves.

For more than twenty years, my wife and I owned as many as four Christian bookstores, and we put our money where our mouth is: we sold only the King James Bible and there were no other versions on our shelves. Either we were crazy, which is one viable option, or we were caring and convicted.

Please withhold your final judgement until you read the material and think it through.

One problem we may have, you and I, is that you are prejudiced against believing any Bible, much less just one, just the King James. And when your prejudices run afoul of my convictions, sparks may fly. From my side, every effort will be made to avoid being pedantic and dogmatic. Rather, you will read names, dates, places, and compare verses, so that you can corroborate the material and come to your own conclusion.

By the way, prejudiced belief in favor of the King James Bible is just as unacceptable as being prejudiced against it. It is facts we need, not fables or favoritism.

In fact, don't you dare take the "King James position" because of what another person teaches or believes. Rather, do as Paul instructs:

"Study to shew thyself approved unto God" (II Timothy 2: 15).

"My people are destroyed for lack of knowledge" (Hosea 4:6).

Follow the pattern of the Thessalonians that Paul so admired when he wrote "For this cause also thank we God without ceasing, because, when ye received the word of God which ye heard of us, ye received it not as the word of men, but as it is in truth, the word of God, which effectually worketh also in you that believe." (I Thessalonians 2:13)

What follows is some information for you to study, some knowledge for you to assimilate, some truth that will work effectually in you that believe:

however, study carefully and independently in order that you become fully persuaded in your own mind. (Romans 14:5)

The fact that you like your fried chicken cooked one way and I prefer another illustrates how difficult it is to get Christians to agree on anything. Should the toilet paper roll be put on the fixture with the lead sheet against the wall or toward the front? Should the plants be watered in the morning or at dusk?

And so it is even more difficult to get Christians to agree on doctrinal matters, particularly controversial doctrinal matters that require deep, detailed and often difficult study.

But let us make the attempt and do so by starting at the very beginning with the most basic and elementary items. By initiating our study with that which is very simple and foundational, at least we can start out nodding in the same direction and then we will see how long that lasts.

Can we agree that God inspired the Bible and that the Bible is God's word?

While it is true that there are whole Christian church denominations and millions of other people who do not believe the Bible is God's word, the point of agreement at which I would start with you is that of believing that God inspired the Bible.

As a matter of fact, you have in Acts 1:16 a most amazing verse which declares that "this scripture (the words of God, no less) must needs have been fulfilled, which the Holy Ghost by the mouth of David spake." David was a murderer, a fornicator, a disobedient king at the very least; and if you had seen him speaking, you would have been witness to God the Holy Spirit speaking through David. What matters, then, is God's word and not the human instrumentations God used during the process of inspiring His Bible.

It's amazing! God wrote the Bible. (Here is where we both nod affirmatively and start to dig in to this study).

The ten dollar word for what we are thinking

about just now is "textual criticism" which is the discipline by which scholars determine which part of the Bible is, in fact, God's word. The Lord Himself has some things to say on the subject:

Jehovah God gives the prophet Jeremiah very specific instructions with respect to the transmission of God's words in Jeremiah 36:2 when God says "Take thee a roll of a book, and write therein all the words that I have spoken unto thee against Israel".

In Ezekiel 1:3 we read "The word of the LORD came expressly unto Ezekiel the priest." There are dozens of additional examples which could be cited, but we have both already nodded affirmatively that God did, in fact, write the Bible by inspiration.

Some might say that William Shakespeare was inspired when he wrote his great plays. For more than ten years I wrote more than fifty newspaper columns each year and people generous with their praise sometimes told me that what I had written was inspired. God's inspiration, however, is entirely different from the general application of the word.

II Timothy 3:16 states that "All scripture is given by inspiration of God, and is profitable for doctrine, for reproof, for correction, for instruction in righteousness:" and we have all heard, at one time or another, that "inspiration" here comes from a Greek word meaning "God breathed."

God Himself put it into men to write down God's words exactly as God wanted with the result being that "Man shall not live by bread alone, but by every word that proceedeth out of the mouth of God," (Matthew 4:4) and "He that rejecteth me, and receiveth not my words, hath one that judgeth him: the word that I have spoken, the same shall judge him in the last day. (John 12:48)

If God did not inspire His word and make it available, from whence cometh faith, since "faith cometh by hearing, and hearing by the word of God." (Romans 10:17) We could never show ourselves approved unto God had God not provided His perfect word to rightly divide. (II Timothy 2:15). This may sound impertinent, but it is only intended to make a point: if God did not give us His word He would have to call off the judgement seat of Christ because it would be unfair to judge our works without our having access to His words. "For the prophecy came not in old time by the will of man but holy men of God spake as they were moved by the Holy Ghost." (II Peter 1:21)

And so we have verse, after verse, after verse telling us that the word of God is inspired and written by God, even though it might have been Peter, or Jeremiah, or James, or Ezekiel, or Paul who was actually inscribing the words.

There is good reason to believe that Paul had eye trouble and used an amanuensis to write words God inspired Paul to give to his secretary. And the fact that no one can really be certain who authored the book of Hebrews makes the point that human authorship does not really matter: God wrote the Bible.

God got the words written down for mankind to read in the form that God wanted man to have. And the original writings, often called the original manuscripts or the original autographs, came into existence by the hand of humanity; but deity inspired each and every word with perfect precision.

Holy Writ, the canon of scripture, call it what you will: God's word is what we are talking about.

Remember Acts 1:16? "Men and brethren, this scripture must needs have been fulfilled, which the Holy Ghost by the mouth of David spake…"

Did we not learn from that passage that the real issue is not about the men involved but rather God's inspiration? Oftentimes people get greatly invested in the human authorship of each book and seem to forget that it is God's words, not the words of men. Great debates, for example, have been waged over the human authorship of Hebrews or the cultural setting for Paul's writings, but let us never forget that it is God who inspired His Bible.

What we are studying is called the doctrine of

inspiration, and there are millions of people who believe in it and millions who do not; but we have agreed at the outset that God did, in fact, write the Bible.

Here, however, we must address a point about which we may part company: where is God's word today? Given that God inspired His words twenty to thirty-four centuries ago, utilizing more than forty different authors, where can we find God's words today?

Most every church, denomination, seminary, or Bible institute has a statement of faith, and generally the first article of such a statement is about the word of God. Almost universally they state that the institution believes that God's word is perfect and inerrant, in the original manuscripts.

That my be what you believe.

However, there are no original manuscripts. Not even one. All we have are copies of copies and more copies, numbering into the thousands; but no originals have ever been discovered.

More than five thousand six hundred manuscripts for just the New Testament exist and many if not most of them differ one from another.

More than 5,600 manuscripts but no originals	
80+	Papyrus fragments from 2nd to 7th centuries
260+	Capital letter (majuscules) mss. from 4th to 10th centuries
2700+	Small letter (miniscule) mss. from 9th to 16th centuries
2200+	Lesson books, sermon books, lectionaries, etc.
1100+	Manuscripts for the four gospels
350+	Manuscripts for Acts and the General Epistles
600+	Manuscripts for Paul's Epistles
200+	Manuscripts for Revelation

Hundreds of translations of the New Testament exist in dozens of languages, and they all differ one from another.

No single English translation matches any single Greek translation, no, not even one.

And so, what are we to do? Was God's word only inerrant, inspired and perfect in those originals which are long gone and long lost?

And if we do not have God's inerrant, inspired and perfect words, how do we know if we are saved or lost? How do we know with certainly what workmanship would not be shameful and what constitutes acceptable service?

If we do not have the originals of the ten commandments, should we be open to the ten commandments media maven and atheist Ted Turner wrote back in the nineties? You might say that God's commandments would be the ones to follow, but without the inspired, inerrant and perfect original manuscripts available, how do you know that for certain? We might agree that God wrote the Bible by inspiration and we may not move one inch from that position; but where is God's perfect word right this minute?

Since we do not have any of the original manuscripts, there are those who would say that what we do have might not be perfect, but that it is pretty good. J. Vernon McGee taught Bible lessons on the radio for decades and his statement was that no Bible we can read today is perfect, but some are "right close."

The other side of the coin would be those who would say that inerrant means inerrant and perfect means perfect and that nothing short of that is acceptable when we are talking about God's words.

My position would be that the difference between the person who rejects or corrects even one word in God's Bible and the atheist who rejects every word in God's Bible is only a matter of degree: both are infidels. And you can be certain that the man who starts out correcting just one word will end up correcting many, many more.

Perhaps, were the point pressed, you would admit that you think the word Easter in Acts 12:4 is a mistake and should have been translated Passover because every Greek manuscript ever located says pascha, the word for Passover.

Gotcha.

If you would change one word (Easter) you are on the slippery slope to total infidelity toward God's words.

And while it is true that every manuscript ever found for the book of Acts says pascha, since we do not have the originals that Luke penned, we must confine our debate over this apparent error to what we do have.

And what we do have is incontrovertible proof that Passover would be a wrong translation.

Note: Acts 12:3: And because he saw it pleased the Jews, he proceeded further to take Peter also. (Then were the days of unleavened bread.)

Since unleavened bread comes after Passover, Acts 12:3 proves that pascha/Passover is simply wrong.

Leviticus 23:5-6: In the fourteenth day of the first month at even is the LORD's passover. And on the fifteenth day of the same month is the feast of unleavened bread unto the LORD: seven days ye must eat unleavened bread.

The person who says that most of the Bible is accurate but there are some mistakes in it obligates himself to making a list of those mistakes so that we can fix them. But with no originals, how would we verify which part of the Bible was correct and which part was in error? If you have fallen into the tender trap of tampering with God's perfect words because of scholarship and state-of-the-art preaching and teaching, at least recognize your infidelity for what it is.

Depicted here are four martyrs being burned at the stake because they owned and read the Bible.

The two most frequently attacked verses in the King James Bible

Acts 12:4 And when he had apprehended him, he put him in prison, and delivered him to four quaternions of soldiers to keep him; intending after Easter to bring him forth to the people.	"Easter" is said to be a mistake and every Greek mss. reads "pascha" which is Passover. The KJ borrowed "Easter" from Martin Luther's Bible because no Greek manuscript ever found is correct in the face of Acts 12:3 cross-referred to Leviticus 23:5-6. Since we have no original mss. and since no Greek mss. adheres to the order of the feasts, the King James translators produced an accurate Bible although as a translation, it does not match any Greek text.
I John 5:7 For there are three that bear record in heaven, the Father, the Word, and the Holy Ghost: and these three are one.	The misinformation that this verse is not found in any Greek mss. and was added by late copyists as a gloss, is now a myth with an anti-Trinitarian agenda that has been accepted as fact by most people. This verse, often called the Johannine Comma, is found in the following Greek mss.: #61, #88, #629 and Codex Ravianus. Further, it was quoted in 250 AD by Cyprian, Spanish Bishop Priscillian before 385 AD, Idacius Clarus and Cassadorious in the fourth and fifth centuries and Facundus in the sixth century.

Most every Christian is taught to think that the Greek text is superior to the King James English; and one of the more popular tactics of Bible correcting trickery comes from the book of John.

Agapao, agapao, phileo.

We are told that the Greek gives us better understanding of the Lord's three-time questioning of Peter and that the Lord had to come down to Peter's level the third time He asked the question, Lovest thou me?

John 21:15-17: So when they had dined, Jesus saith to Simon Peter, Simon, son of Jonas, lovest thou me more than these? He saith unto him, Yea, Lord; thou knowest that I love thee. He saith unto him, Feed my lambs. He saith to him again the second time, Simon, son of Jonas, lovest thou me? He saith unto him, Yea, Lord; thou knowest that I love thee. He saith unto him, Feed my sheep. He saith unto him the third time, Simon, son of Jonas, lovest thou me? Peter was grieved because he said unto him the third time, Lovest thou me? And he said unto him, Lord, thou knowest all things; thou knowest that I love thee. Jesus saith unto him, Feed my sheep.

The venerable J. Vernon McGee in his Thru the Bible Commentary says each question is different and that the Lord starts out asking Peter about the highest and most noble level of love (agapao) but the third time the Lord comes down to Peter's more carnal level.

Why, then, does the Bible say in both Greek and King James English that "He saith unto him the third time"? If what we were all told about this passage at one time or another were true, should not the Bible say "Then the Lord tried something different?"

Giving God the benefit of the doubt as opposed to trusting scholarship or popular preaching and teaching will restore fidelity to God's word and the only thing it will cost you is membership in the Union of Bible Denying Bible Correcting Bible Corruptors.

God wrote the Bible, and He did it by direct inspiration.

God inspired His word using nine methods including (1) speaking directly to people as in Exodus 19:19: And when the voice of the trumpet sounded long, and waxed louder and louder, Moses spake, and God answered him by a voice.

God spoke to people in visions (2) which is what takes place in the sixth chapter of Isaiah and some were given God's words in dreams (3) as Matthew 1:20: But while he thought on these things, behold, the angel of the Lord appeared unto him in a dream, saying, Joseph, thou son of David, fear not to take unto thee Mary thy wife: for that which is conceived in her is of the Holy Ghost.

There were times when angels spoke (4) God's words on His behalf as Acts 7:38: This is he, that was in the church in the wilderness with the angel which spake to him in the mount Sina, and with our fathers: who received the lively oracles to give unto us:

Prophets (5) such as Jeremiah and Ezekiel cited earlier disseminated God's word as verified in Hebrews 1:1: God, who at sundry times and in divers manners spake in time past unto the fathers by the prophets,

Apostles (6) spoke and wrote God's words and we know that from Acts 1:2: Until the day in which he was taken up, after that he through the Holy Ghost had given commandments unto the apostles whom he had chosen:

Inspiration (7) is the method cited in II Timothy 3:16: All scripture is given by inspiration of God, and is profitable for doctrine, for reproof, for correction, for instruction in righteousness: as is revelation (8) in II Corinthians 12:1: It is not expedient for me doubtless to glory. I will come to visions and revelations of the Lord.

Finally, God manifest in the flesh, the Lord Jesus Christ Himself (9) presented God's words from God manifest in the flesh: Hebrews 1:2: Hath in these last days spoken unto us by his Son, whom he hath appointed heir of all things, by whom also he made the worlds; Each and every one of the 788,258 words in my King James Bible is the exact word God gave me to study and it is perfect, without error.

When I open my Bible, my attitude toward God's word is the attitude God wants me to have toward His word: I Thessalonians 2:13: ... ye received it not as the word of men, but as it is in truth, the word of God, which effectually worketh also in you that believe.

Are we still in agreement that God wrote the Bible? That is the doctrine of inspiration.

Can we agree that we have God's word in our

language today? That is the doctrine of preservation.

We know from God's word what God wants from us. That is the doctrine of utilization.

God wants us to walk in newness of life: Romans 6:4: Therefore we are buried with him by baptism into death: that like as Christ was raised up from the dead by the glory of the Father, even so we also should walk in newness of life.

God would have me remember that I deserve hell and as a result I am told I Thessalonians 5:18: In every thing give thanks: for this is the will of God in Christ Jesus concerning you.

God saves souls by grace through faith in the finished work of Jesus Christ and that information comes from God's word as in Ephesians 1:13: In whom ye also trusted, after that ye heard the word of truth, the gospel of your salvation: in whom also after that ye believed, ye were sealed with that holy Spirit of promise. The faith came from His word as well: Romans 10:17: So then faith cometh by hearing, and hearing by the word of God.

Our need to use the words of God in the details of our daily lives is this doctrine which I call utilization; and that speaks to the practicality of what is otherwise a discussion of the more esoteric issues of inspiration and preservation.

If the critics and correctors are right when they say God's word was inerrant and perfect only in the original manuscripts, then I was right earlier when I said we could call off the Judgment Seat of Christ.. After all, God would be totally unfair to judge our service and mete out rewards based on the content of a book to which we never had access. How could we obey II Timothy 2:15: Study to shew thyself approved unto God, a workman that needeth not to be ashamed, rightly dividing the word of truth...without access to the word of truth?

God would have a preacher to preach and a teacher to teach God's word, not books from the seminary or thoughts from some commentary.

It is apparent that quite of bit of preaching

and teaching are, in fact, bereft of Bible, but that would be a wrong thing and not a desirable pattern. Quite a considerable portion of contemporary preaching and teaching is little more than the advancement of social, moral or political agendas. Some messages sound more like book reviews than Bible; others are personal experiences masquerading as spirituality.

Many a preacher has a library loaded with sermon books, lectionaries, books of illustrations; and they will combine elements from several such sources and call the result their sermon. For such message preparation, the Bible is unnecessary.

Preaching and teaching are to utilize God's word which we can do because God preserved that which He inspired so that we can confidently and unequivocally declare God's words of God's truth.

My final authority is the word of God, but unlike most people who may say those same exact words, I actually have a copy of God's words. He inspired it: He preserved it: I utilize it.

We are enjoined by God to study; and Jesus twice said that every word matters:

Matthew 4:4: But he answered and said, It is written, Man shall not live by bread alone, but by every word that proceedeth out of the mouth of God.

Luke 4:4: And Jesus answered him, saying, It is written, That man shall not live by bread alone, but by every word of God.

Luke writes in Acts 17:11 about a crowd of people who were more noble than those in Thessalonica simply because they were Bible students. He was speaking of the Bereans, "in that they received the word with all readiness of mind and searched the scriptures daily."

Again, we determined at the outset to start in agreement that God wrote the Bible, that the doctrine of inspiration. We study, preach, teach and adhere to the teachings of the Bible, and that would be the doctrine of utilization.

The absolutely necessary bridge between the

inspiration of the Bible writers and utilization today by Bible readers is the doctrine of preservation, and here is where you and I may part company.

But without preservation, of what real value is inspiration? Without preservation how does one evaluate utilization?

To get from inspiration, where Peter, James, and John were walking around on planet Earth, to utilization, where you and I are walking around on planet Earth, we have to cross a bridge of time with God's word intact.

God has obligated Himself to the doctrine of preservation, the bridge doctrine that no seminary teaches and few preachers or teachers believe.

The Bible, if it is to be believed, teaches the doctrine of preservation, much to the chagrin of the Bible correcting, Bible rejecting, Greek worshiping seminary professors everywhere.

God's pure words were preserved by God Himself:

Psalms 12:6-7: The words of the LORD are pure words: as silver tried in a furnace of earth, purified seven times. Thou shalt keep them, O LORD, thou shalt preserve them from this generation for ever.

Seven purifications: would that be seven thousand years of human history? Might it be the seven English translations: Wycliffe, Matthews, Tyndale, Coverdale, Great, Geneva and Bishop's? It doesn't really matter because the result is God preserves His pure words.

Psalms 119:89: For ever, O LORD, thy word is settled in heaven.

Isaiah 40:8: The grass withereth, the flower fadeth: but the word of our God shall stand for ever.

Jesus said, "For verily I say unto you, Till heaven and earth pass, one jot or one tittle shall in no wise pass from the law, till all be fulfilled" Matthew 5: 18.

Heaven and earth shall pass away but my word shall not pass away. Matthew 24:35.

I Peter 1:25: But the word of the Lord endureth for ever. And this is the word which by the gospel is preached unto you.

The God who spoke worlds into existence spoke His words into existence as well; and we need to use God's words in our lives each and every day.

Inspiration.

Utilization.

Impossible without preservation. The doctrine to which you are now being exposed, this business of preservation, turns out to be of the utmost importance because without preservation, inspiration is of no practical value and utilization becomes impossible.

Because the Bible is critical to the Christian faith, preservation is clearly critical to getting the Christian faith right.

And so, we need to understand how God preserved His word from the time of its inspiration to our time of utilization.

Just as there are many viewpoints with respect to inspiration of God's word and just as there are many out-workings of God's word in practical utilization of its content, we are going to find that this business of preservation is also a bit complex.

Let's start early-on, and try to keep it simple.

In the garden of Eden (and it would be hard to get more early-on than that), the devil himself worked at undermining humanity's faith in God's words.

Genesis 3:1...Yea, hath God said...?

More than four thousand years later, the devil's tactic had not changed:

II Corinthians 2:17: For we are not as many, which corrupt the word of God: but as of sincerity, but as of God, in the sight of God speak we in Christ.

Underline the word "many" in your thinking so that you consider the object of the devilish onslaught which continues to this day: "Yea, hath God said?" Science, major media, public education, entertainment moguls all pose the same question:

"Yea, hath God said?"

To illustrate II Corinthians 2:17, had you gone to a first century Christian bookstore just after the apostle Paul had written his second letter to the people at Corinth, you would have found many corrupted versions of God's word; and even then it would have been a challenge to be certain you had the right one.

Of course there weren't any Christian bookstores back then, but there were churches and there were choices that needed to be made between God's word and Satan's corruptions.

God Himself warns against corrupting His word in His books of the law, in His books of writings, and in prophecy.

Deuteronomy 4:2 (in the law): Ye shall not add unto the word which I command you, neither shall ye diminish ought from it, that ye may keep the commandments of the LORD your God which I command you.

Proverbs 30:6 (in the writings): Add thou not unto his words, lest he reprove thee, and thou be found a liar.

Revelation 22:18 (in prophetic writings): For I testify unto every man that heareth the words of the prophecy of this book, If any man shall add unto these things, God shall add unto him the plagues that are written in this book.

Three warnings in scripture about adding to God's word or deleting from it or both: since we already knew that God's words would be pure and perfect, with these three warnings we have the information we need to identify God's words when we find them.

Clearly, if Paul wrote a letter and there were many corrupted copies of it, corruption would have had more availability than the pure words of scripture. And so, as we dig in to our study, we can already see that Satan himself put questioning God's word to Eve in the garden by offering her a corruption of what God had said; and those devilish tactics persist and were born witness to by the apostle

Paul.

Also, we do well to remember that "every man at his best state is altogether vanity" (Psalm 39:5) and man would much rather worship himself than his creator (Romans 1:25). When confronted with the words of God, humanity undermines its authority, ultimately replacing God's words with humanistic philosophy.

"Yea, hath God said," indeed. Nothing changes: everything stays the same.

Eve said in Genesis 3:3: "'But of the fruit of the tree which is in the midst of the garden, God hath said, Ye shall not eat of it, [That's true.] neither shall ye touch it" [That's not true.]

The devil sowed seeds of doubt and Eve bit, not the proverbial apple, (more likely a grape), but infidelity to what God had said. Eve then misled the devil about the Word of God: she lied about what God's words actually were.

Also, Eve left out the word "freely," and humanity continues to this very day to try to work his way to heaven rather than to trust what God provided "freely" through Calvary's cross.

As we study the preservation of God's words we know what to watch for because we know the devil's tactics: God's words will be corrupted by adding to them, deleting from them and by lying about the doctrines the words contain.

From the corruption of Paul's letters in the first century after the cross of Christ, we will now follow both the trail of corruption and the tracks of purity as we proceed.

Remember, the words of scripture did not simply begin in the minds of the writers of scripture, but rather, in the mind of God Himself. We may think of William Shakespeare as having been inspired, or Ernest Hemingway, or Ezra Pound. We may have lucid moments in our own life experience when we might even say we, our own selves, had been inspired.

That, however, is not the kind of inspiration to which the Bible refers.

The words of the Bible did not simply begin as thoughts in the synapses of human brains but rather were put into the human realm by God's direct intervention.

"God-breathed" is often how inspiration is described by churchmen, but there is more to it than even that. We know, for example, that Paul wrote material that is not in the Bible and that Paul quotes from unsaved authors, which means that God was putting his Bible together apart from simple human instrumentation. God also selected certain writings from particular authors and rejected others. It was not merely God's providing enlightenment; but according to God's purposes for His words, God's words are accurate, even when the Bible quotes people telling lies, as Peter's denial of the Lord.

Since God wrote the Bible, as we chose to agree (or at least consider) early on, we now see that this subject is both important and complicated; but at least we know we are looking for God's pure words, uncorrupted by humanity, available to all people.

God's inspired words first showed up as letters or books or proverbs or psalms written down on the paper of their time, generally parchment.

What Moses or Paul or David or Peter wrote down would be referred to as "original manuscripts," but none of those original manuscripts has ever been found. The perplexity of the problem that promulgates is that without the originals we are on a search for which copies, which translations, which lectionaries, which song books might contain the most accurate rendering of what God said.

Two important issues come to mind at this juncture: firstly, every preacher or teacher quoting the "originals" is either ignorant or deceptive as there are no originals; and the ignorant and the deceptive are not worthy of our attention as we study.

Secondly, since there are no originals to backstop and verify the conclusion we come to as a result of study, we will require a great deal of corroboration in order to become fully persuaded in our own minds. Getting that information is why this book has been made available.

The inspired words of God along with all the other words God wanted included in His Bible, right down to the words that came out of the mouth of Job's wife ("Curse God and die." Job 2:9), all started out written down using the writing materials of their day.

Silly though this may sound, perhaps a fisherman such as Peter had terrible penmanship and couldn't spell well. That would be one good reason why God might not be particularly interested in the original manuscripts. Another might be that, were the originals found, they would be in the center ring of some museum's circle of artifacts and you would have to buy a ticket to catch a glimpse.

Copies of manuscripts were produced so that more and more people could hear and read the contents, yet many more corruptions were simultaneously being produced.

Because corruption of that which had been pure was an issue since the garden and clearly in place in the first century, it was incumbent upon those copying that which was right to do a good job of it. The copyist, then, operated with fear and trembling in his heart and skill and precision in his fingers as he produced exact copies of God's exact words. Respect for God's words was under-girded by the desire to avoid having the Lord "take away his part out of the book of life, and out of the holy city" (Revelation 22:19).

And the Lord Himself did not have forty-two men write more than three quarters of a million words over a fourteen hundred year period of time just to lose those same words and have human scholars and professors do the best they could at giving their best guess at what God said.

So there it was: God's words as originally written in three languages on the materials used for writing twenty and more centuries ago, copied and copied and copied.

Christianity is not an oral tradition but a faith

based on a book; and that book even goes so far as to say that "faith cometh by hearing, and hearing by the word of God." (Romans 10:17) and that "without faith, it is impossible to please God." (Hebrews 11:6) That means we need to care very much about having the right book, the book that is God's word. The Hebrew language is what God used for most of the Old Testament. Jesus is quoted speaking Aramaic, and a small portion of the Old Testament is in that language. The New Testament is written in the common Greek of the people, referred to as Koine Greek, not the classical or priest class Greek, but the more common.

Copies were made, as were corruptions.

And as we move away from the cross and leave the first century and the time of the apostles, we come to the time referred to as Ante-Nicene.

The "Nicene" part refers to the Council of Nicea, held in 325 A.D. Since "ante" means before, historians would name and frame the time we now study as being before the Council of Nicea.

You will hear of Christian leaders who lived before 325 A.D. referred to as ante-Nicene Fathers.

From this, it should jump off the page to your cognition that such description would be Roman Catholic in orientation, as they would use the term "Father" but no saved person would.

These men had names and wrote books, so you can look them up, read their books, and decide for yourself if you would accept them as reliable. No one, however, would confuse them with the apostles and prophets, and no one would look at the ante-Nicene Father's writings as being scripture.

Read Irenaeus or Hippolytus and you will see their erudition and you may even find their ancient texts interesting as did I; and it would be a good thing to have a level of familiarity with these so-called Fathers because of their significance to the written traditions and witnesses to Christianity, both to the pure and to the corrupt.

While we are at it, by the way, keep in mind

that there only need be one that is pure, while corruption never knows any limits; and we know there were many corrupt even in the first century.

Large numbers of those living prior to the Council of Nicea were called upon to exhibit great courage. Just as we have some historical reasons to believe that the apostles were tortured and murdered, similarly, first and second century believers often suffered persecution. Christ had been crucified, and those who opposed Christ lived to tell about it while many believers did not: again we see reason to understand why the corrupt is more pervasive than the pure.

What is truly confounding is that during that time frame before the Council of Nicea there were people calling themselves Christians who were corrupting the words of God for their own purposes and some people who called themselves Christians were even killing other people who called themselves Christians.

There were people calling themselves Christians hiding under the city of Rome in a system of tunnels called the catacombs. People in Rome, also calling themselves Christians, wanted to feed those that were hiding to the lions.

Those people hiding attached great importance to the words of God as they had little else. The people doing the attacking were more oriented toward power and politics, which helps us better understand what took place in 325 A.D. at the Council of Nicea.

That is an amazing thing to consider, but understand that people who were hiding in the catacombs, under the city of Rome in a network of secret passages that went on for miles, had a faith in the Lord Jesus Christ and they had their Bibles. These people were being killed by other people, largely pagans, but soon to be also those that called themselves Christians.

This might be a propitious time for reading <u>Foxe's Book of Christian Martyrs</u> to become familiar with the blood-bought price the early believers had to pay at the hands of those wicked and heathen people who murdered under their flag of Christianity.

Some of those early Christians were most amazing people of courage and character.

Imagine, if you can, not even being allowed to die a martyr's death with dignity. Instead, you might be doused with oil, chained to a stake and set afire to illuminate those of your brethren who would be fed to the lions. Yet the irony of being a source of light burning in the parapets of the arena should not be lost on us as we continue to be the only source for a different sort of light to a lost and dying world.

Still, imagine.

Instead of being fed to lions or fighting one another with some semblance of dignity, consider having a leather bag over your body all the way down to your knees, your hands chained behind your back. Blinded by the bag, hindered by the handcuffing, wandering around without direction to the laughter and cat calls of the audience, many of whom referred to themselves as Christians. One more thing: in the bag with you were poisonous serpents, against whom you were defenseless. You might run or roll or hit yourself against a wall you happened against, but your death would be anonymous and without pity.

Another book, <u>Martyr's Mirror</u>, probably belongs in your library.

This was an amazing time when people who really cared about God's words were being murdered by people who wanted to manipulate God's words to control others, using power and politics.

It is in this context that the battle between the pure text and the corrupted was joined. The blood-bought church with its blood-bought Bible constituted the tiny minority, while the powerful protected their own interests.

The ante-Nicene Fathers were not all bad, but it is hard to think many of them were saved people. Some of their writings are pure heresy, others thought-provoking, some others profound, while some seem silly. Against this confusing background, we move into the second century and encounter a most significant figure in the history of Christian thought.

This was a man of unquestioned intellect who was considered without peer by his contemporaries; and although he called himself a Christian, in fact he was not a believer.

He did not believe that Jesus Christ was God in the flesh, (Colossians 2:9: ...the fulness of the Godhead bodily), and he did not accept the miracles reported in scripture as being actual events.

This man's name is easy to remember because he is the origin of a style of textual criticism that denigrates the deity of Christ, he is the origin of treating the Bible as being anti-intellectual, he is the origin of explaining away God's miracles, he is the origin of so very much that is wrong; and, his name is Origen, Adamantius Origen.

Origen was born in 184 AD and died at seventy, which took his influence midway into the third century. His doctrine would be very close to the belief system of today's Jehovah's Witness, particularly holding that Christ was not God, or at best, a lesser God.

Perhaps Origen's mind was so complex that he was more easily traduced into error in that he trusted his mind over the Bible, and thus, he outsmarted himself. Some of his books are still in print so you can read what he had to say and note his brilliance as a scholar. He was wrong, he believed and taught heresy; but his scholarship and his mind were fabulous.

Intellect alone caused Adamantius Origen to be ensconced as the head of the Gnostic School of Christianity, gnostics being the "wiser ones" and Origen being their head.

If you are an agnostic, that words means you don't know something and find that acceptable, even laudable. Gnostics applaud knowing, and the leader of the gnostics in the third century was this brilliant man who did not believe the Bible's miracles or that Jesus Christ was in fact God.

Such a man would hardly be who you might select to translate and transmit God's word, but that is exactly what Adamantius Origen did.

The belief system of Adamantius Origen included:
Baptismal regeneration, including infant baptism
Universalism, including salvation of the Devil
Purgatory followed by reincarnation of the soul
Jesus as a created being
Adam, Eve and Creation as being mythical
Communion being the real presence of Christ (transubstantiation)

The most famous and influential book that Origen compiled is called the Hexapala. Just as a hexagon has six sides, Origen's Hexapala had six columns of text, each one a Bible translation either written or edited by Origen himself.

The fifth column of the Hexapala was an original New Testament translation produced by Origen, a work that would turn out to be one of the most significant literary works in all human history.

An audience was already in place for Origen's deity-denying miracle-minimizing work in that before Origen was born, the Alexandrian School of Religion and Philosophy was already in place, producing theological leaders. There resided the people who did not accept the existence of heaven or hell and ridiculed those who took the Bible literally.

When the translators associated with the Alexandrian School worked with Bible manuscripts they made changes according to their unbelief in Christ's deity, unbelief in Bible miracles, unbelief in heaven and hell. These would be the sorts of people that Paul warned about in II Corinthians 2:17: For we are not as many, which corrupt the word of God: but as of sincerity, but as of God, in the sight of God speak we in Christ.

The arrogance of changing God's word to

match human unbelief or a humanistic agenda may seem extreme; however, the pattern was set by Eve in Genesis as she adjusted God's words to suit herself. Note the timing and follow the progression: in the first century Paul said many were corrupting the word of God, in the second century the Alexandrian school was in place and the Gnostic School and Origen by the third century. The Council of Nicea was 325 AD which is early-on in the fourth century, which means we have chronicled nearly four centuries of infidelity and tampering with the text of God's word.

Separate and apart from that, the true text was in the hands of martyrs willing to die for God's words; and it is important to notice that the corrupted words and God's pure words were both in place and being preserved simultaneously. We will see that the two streams of manuscripts, corrupted and pure, are still in place and are still competing for attention to this very day: at this point we have seen how the two streams of manuscripts started out and how they were clearly both in place during the Ante-Nicene epoch.

Scholars and historians consider the Council of Nicea to be a benchmark event in the progression of Christianity, and no doubt it was. Not only did the Nicene Creed emanate from the Council of Nicea, so did the paganization of Christianity as a result of the leadership of the Emperor Constantine.

As a sun worshiper, Constantine claimed to see a vision instructing him to conquer the world with the symbol of a cross on the soldier's shields and a sword in their hand.

Those soldiers, by the way, became "Christians" by marching under trees in which were "baptizers" with buckets of water in the branches of the trees, dousing the troops below.

The cross of Constantine's vision did not look like the cross of Calvary but rather like the Ankh of Egyptian sun worship. Constantine said that God had told him: "In this sign, conquer." An ankh looks like a capital letter "T" with a circular sun-worship symbol on top. (Ankhs are a popular jewelry item, almost always included in catalogs such as Avon's).

Constantine declared himself to be a Christian just as a cow could declare itself to be a sparrow; but you know which you would prefer to fly over your freshly washed car, and it wouldn't be the cow. By the way, you may call yourself a Christian, but if your faith is not in Christ's payment for your sins, by grace and through faith alone in Christ alone, that flying cow has more chance of getting into heaven than do you.

Like most unsaved church members today, Constantine's faith was in water baptism rather than in Christ; but Constantine added a different wrinkle: the Emperor wanted to be baptized when he was on his deathbed so that the maximum number of sins could be "washed away".

The Emperor Constantine presided over the Council of Nicea with his sword-bearing army freshly baptized and ready to conquer in the sign of paganized Christianity. All of this information is available, although as the years go by more and more of the materials included in this book's bibliography go out of print. The internet can help, but the best and most reliable source is still books such as one entitled <u>Constantine</u> published by MacMillan; and you will find this incredible information about Constantine on pages seventy-two through one hundred-twelve.

Emperor Constantine may well have been the first Pope in that Peter certainly was not; and it was Constantine who referred to himself as the Summis Pontifex, the official title of the papacy. The apostle Peter had a wife, a mother-in-law, children, and refused to let people worship or adore him: very un-pope-like.

Constantine, however, was a religionist trusting water baptism combined with secular power: very pope-like.

For our purposes, however, the most important thing about the Emperor was the significant part he played in the preservation and transmission of the corrupted and counterfeited scriptures.

While neither a scholar nor a translator, Constantine did respect the need for intellectual pursuits. After all, the Alexandrian School of the second century and the Gnostic School of the third century had served as precursors to the Council of Nicea in the fourth century. It was logical, then, that Constantine commissioned the production of fifty Bibles.

Not parchment, but rolled out hides from fair skinned antelopes would be the writing material and the very best calligraphers were to do the work. Every page would have the same number of lines and the capital letters starting books would be works of art.

At this time, the pure text of the blood-bought church was being protected by the martyrs, being hidden in the Catacombs, being removed to safer locales. No blood-bought believer had anything to do with a Summis Pontifex in those days, unlike our foolishly ecumenical orientation today. The Emperor did not go to the martyrs for the pure words of God; rather, Constantine had the corrupted text of Origen's fifth column copied fifty times in durable and beautiful volumes called codices. The scholar Eusebius of the Gnostic school was commissioned by Constantine, and Eusebius selected Origen's text. Those fifty Bibles were in the ecclesiastical Greek language and very likely constitute the texts of the fourth century Vaticanus and Siniaticus.

To Eusebius and his Emperor, this was all most logical; and the Council of Nicea validated that thinking. What we recognize, however, is that the corrupted text of II Corinthians 2:17 had matriculated through the Alexandrian School, the Gnostic School and then the Council of Nicea, at the behest of a baptismal regenerate who called himself the Summis Pontifex. The corrupted Greek text was in position to exert tremendous influence, and so it did and so it still does.

The pure words of God were still available,

still being read and studied, but by declining numbers of people who were being murdered in the Coliseums. Eventually, Roman Catholicism would slaughter between forty-four and sixty-eight million people with the beginnings of the mayhem under the Emperor Constantine's reign as he conquered under the sign of the ankh.

Wonderful books have been written which document all of this information in exquisite detail; and you would do well to start by reading everything you can get your hands on by Dr. David Otis Fuller, Dr. Edward Hills, and Dean Burgeon.

Suffice it to say that you are able to clearly chronicle corruption seeping forward through centuries of time. The foundations for the Roman Catholic Church, paganized Christianity, and corrupted Bibles were solidly in place.

Jerome's Latin Vulgate Bible came directly from the fifty Bibles made up by Eusebius from the deity-denying text of Adamantius Origen, meaning that the emerging papist church of Roman Catholicism had a Bible in Latin, making its text virtually inaccessible for the common man who could not read Latin.

Much mischief was to follow.

The Latin Vulgate became the official Bible for the popish people of Roman Catholicism, no doubt the same "popish persons" the King James translators specifically said they wanted to avoid. And with the Bible in Latin and the sword in the hands of the Summis Pontifex, blood began to flow.

Depending on which source you accept as authoritative, Roman Catholic Popes, priests and nuns killed as many as six times the people that Hitler murdered in his death camps. Yet, against that horrific background, the members of the blood-bought church of the living God, the pillar and ground of truth, had God's Bible in their charge.

Down through the centuries after the Council of Nicea and the emergence of murderous Roman Catholicism, the true believers were outcasts, hunted down and martyred. Often, such groups were identified by names reflective of their leadership: followers of Waldo were called Waldensians, for example. One group with distinctive Pauline dispensational doctrine was called Paulicians, with that name intended to be accusatory and pejorative. Meanwhile, all such groups really cared about was that they were not following the Pope.

These groups preserved a Bible text that had not passed through the hands of the Alexandrian school. Perhaps they knew that nothing good (in the Bible) ever came out of Egypt. Their text had not been perverted by the heresy of Adamantius Origen, attacking the deity of the Lord Jesus Christ. Their text was not welcome at the Council of Nicea.

The die had been cast, the gauntlet had been thrown, the line had been drawn; there were going to be two texts competing for attention: the pure in the hands of the martyrs and the corrupt in the hands of the popish.

The Bible of the true Christians never cross-pollinated with the corrupted texts until the nineteenth century. From the fourth century, where we are now in our study, until the late eighteen hundreds, the issue was fairly simple and easily discerned.

Paul had warned believers of corruption when he wrote II Corinthians as we noted earlier, and the corrupted texts are easily traced into the fourth century.

From the fourth century onward for about one thousand years, as the saying goes, all roads led to Rome; and the issue that most true Christians cared about was not textual criticism. Roman Catholicism, with its corrupted Bible, was crowning kings and ruling over most of the civilized world.

If you were a real Christian with the real Bible, you could be killed for having that Bible and you could be killed for denying the tenants of Romanism.

History books generally refer to this time as the Dark Ages, that terrible time when the church was not separated from the state but in fact controlled the state. That church, however, was the paganized church of the popes and not the blood-bought church of true believers.

This dichotomy of two groups, each referring to themselves as Christians, persists. There are only two groups today, not hundreds of denominations, as the naive might suppose: there is the church of the "Do" and the church of the "Done." Romish, popish groups always require their adherents to do things in order to be or stay saved. That would include, of course, most so-called protestant groups which are almost as Romish and popish as the source of their error: Romanism and its Bible.

The church of the "Done" knows that Jesus Christ did everything necessary for a soul to be saved and our faith in His payment for our sins is sufficient.

During the Dark Ages there were no denominations, no Protestants: there was only Roman Catholicism and the blood-bought believers scattered in small groups, hidden or martyred.

And the Papists had the corrupted text, while the martyrs often died protecting the pure text.

If you have never read an unedited and unabridged copy of Foxe's Book of Martyrs, do not consider yourself to be a "well-read" Christian. You should take the time to wade through Martyr's Mirror. Additionally, when you read that material and learn the bloody history of Roman Catholicism, you will never again think of "Holy Mother Rome" as being beneficent or benevolent. Do not skip over the bibliography at the back of this book, and take note of The Other Side of Rome and similar titles.

When a twenty-first century Pope declared that Roman Catholicism was the only true church, he was not saying anything new. During the Dark Ages, however, if you did not believe that Mary or a priest could intercede for you or if you did not believe that the Pope spoke for God, you could be tortured and killed.

God does not grade sin on a curve but on the cross. Roman Catholicism has long graded sin on a curve: venial (able to be expiated) or mortal (beyond expiation). Believe it or not, in those days it was a mortal sin to read the Bible because so doing undermined the authority of the church. Sixty-eight million is the high estimate of people murdered by priests, nuns and deacon and forty-four million the low estimate. Either is virtually unimaginable, being six to ten times the number killed by Adolf Hitler during World War II. (Hitler and his henchmen, by the way, all were Roman Catholic as well).

What an abomination, all in the name of God!

You may be deluded into thinking that the Roman Catholic church today has changed and you may point to Vatican I and II as proof. If that is what you believe, your thinking demonstrates that you have not read either Vatican I or II, and you should. In those documents you will find the Council of Trent is still efficacious and you will read that Bible-believing Christians saved by God's grace through faith are cursed to eternal damnation more than forty times in Vatican I and II.

During the Inquisitions and the Dark Ages, there were no Christian bookstores selling competing versions of the Bible. There were no denominations putting out their own versions of the Bible with their own spin on both the notes and the translation itself. The issue during that thousand years was staying alive.

One man (chronicled in <u>Foxes Book of Martyrs</u> pages 152-153) rejected the Roman Catholic church, and a contingent of priests demanded that he recant; when he did not, they first beat him and then they tied him up by one arm, then the other, until the shoulders dislocated. They pulled the nails from each finger and each toe, pulled out all his teeth, slit his ears and poured molten lead on his nail-less fingers and toes. Finally, a knotted cord was twisted about his forehead until his skull gave way and his eyes were forced out. The priests wanted his slow tortured death to be a witness to the power of the Roman Catholic church.

Holy Mother Rome indeed: mother of harlots

fits much better; but the point is that during this time there was no Bible version issue.

During the Dark Ages, however, there were two Bibles.

We have already identified the scriptures of the martyrs protected by the Anabaptists, the Anapedabaptists, the Paulicians, the Domitists, and the Waldensens, and a lot of other small groups whose beliefs could cost them their lives.

Roman Catholicism had the Latin Vulgate Bible which we have already traced back through the corruption of Origen, Eusibuis, Constantine and the papacy.

The power of the Popes and Roman Catholicism in world history, is undeniable: Popes set boundaries for countries and crowned their kings.

The corruption of the Popes and Roman Catholicism, historically, are also undeniable: avaricious, homosexual, insane, and greedy for both power and riches. To this day, the most ornate cathedrals with the most jewels and gilt are in the poorest of Roman Catholic countries.

Pope Leo X, in the early sixteenth century, determined to glorify himself and his reign as pope by building a great basilica, which by definition is an oval and opulent building to serve as a seat of rulership.

Construction was scheduled and artisans were being gathered and a massive fund raising effort was mounted, using the tremendous influence and pervasive presence of the Roman Catholic church.

One popular way of raising money was the sale of what were called "indulgences." A person could indulge in sinful behavior and have that sin forgiven when the appropriate price was paid to the Roman Catholic church.

Let's say there was a man who had an eye for the girl next door and was planning to fornicate with her. He could pay the priest and all was forgiven. When the man's wife found out, she could kill her unfaithful husband without consequence,

Ankh

Origen, (above left), produced the text used by Eusibius, (at right), under the first Pope, Summis Pontifex Constantine, (at top).
(Below), Roman Catholic priests burn William Tyndale at the sstke for having produced a Bible in the English language.

-37-

had the wife paid the price for her crime.

Since the government was controlled by the church, payment of indulgences absolved the miscreant completely. The guilty would have purchased forgiveness from the church and the government, and so the corruption of the papacy and priesthood spread to the people, as you would expect. After all, if they had the money they would never have to face jail or even one day in purgatory: they would go straight to heaven and Peter would grant them admission through the pearly gates.

If you are ignorant of the murderous and corrupt history of Roman Catholicism you can be thankful that ignorance is curable with study. Again, use this book's bibliography to your advantage. The Reformation published by TimeLife, covers the sale of indulgences and its primary practitioner, John Tetzel, on pages thirty-six to thirty-nine.

In the early fifteen-hundreds, one Roman Catholic monk was separated from the crowd, probably because that monk was reading a Bible translated from the text that the popes had prohibited, the text of the martyrs.

He was reading a Greek New Testament from Antioch, a Syrian Text, the text of the blood-bought Church, and here he was, part of the murderous Roman Catholic system. Perhaps second only to Saul of Tarsus becoming Paul the apostle, Martin Luther's conversion and convictions are incalculable.

For Luther to read the text of the martyrs would be tantamount to a Christian looking for truth in "The Satanic Bible." Meanwhile, this young Augustinian monk in Germany was an iconoclast even then, and something of a character.

When Martin Luther read in Romans 1:17 that "the just shall live by faith," he knew that he was not. He knew that he was living by sacraments and baptisms and rituals and liturgies. Luther considered that salvation just might be by faith and in his commentaries on Romans and Galatians you can read how he was sorting things out more than five centuries ago.

Luther had been making the sign of the cross on his abdomen, from which we get the expression "cross your fingers and hope to die;" but Martin Luther was beginning to see the only real hope was in the cross of the Lord Jesus Christ.

It is possible to read some of Luther's writings and conclude that he was saved and that he understood the gospel of God's grace; other places you might read and realize there was much that Luther did not comprehend. On every page of Luther's writings, however, you see a man with great personal integrity advancing God's truth as had not been attempted or accomplished for more than ten centuries.

The story goes that Martin Luther wrote 95 objections to John Tetzel's indulgences and nailed them to the door of the Wittenburg church. Actually, the <u>Ninety-Five Theses</u> covered many subjects and were more likely posted just inside Wittenburg's door on a sort of bulletin board. You cannot be "well read" as a Christian if you have not read the <u>Ninety-Five Theses;</u> and when you do, it will be clear to you that Luther was coming out of the Dark Ages and was yet in the dark about many things.

All Hallow's Eve, now corrupted into Hallowe'en, 1517 is when Luther's list was posted.

The famous "shot heard round the world" of the American Revolutionary War would be like a pop gun compared to an atomic blast when contrasted to the influence of Luther and what came to be known as the Reformation.

Secular history points proudly to this period of time as the Renaissance of learning, art and science. Without the Reformation, however, the freedom that the Renaissance required would not have existed. Both the secularistic atheist and the saved Christian are indebted to the courage of this one man who stood with God's word as he found it in the text of the martyrs.

That Luther died in his sleep is amazing. He wrote the pope a letter addressed "Your Hellishness." He attacked the cash-generating indulgence system; and as the years went by, Luther increasingly depended on his Bible which caused him to take more and more positions contrary to the papacy.

It was not called "The Protestant Reformation" back then: it was called dangerous or even a death sentence.

By 1534, however, so much was happening that there was no going back, and the battle for men's minds never would be quite the same. It was during that year that the Jesuit Order was founded by the Roman Catholic church and given the objective of stopping what Luther, or more precisely the Bible of the martyrs, had started.

The Encyclopedia Americana Volume 17, page 673, says, "The purpose of the Jesuit Order founded by Ignatius Loyola was to stop the spread of Protestantism at all costs." The Jesuits engineered a massacre to kill Protestants on August 24, 1572. They used Roman Catholic troops and Dominican monks to do the job. Without so much as a warning, they killed unarmed Christians in Paris. Blood ran thick and hot for almost two weeks.

England was a particularly desirable target for the Jesuit order in that it was fact that the sun never set on the British Empire and so her influence was global. "Britannia ruled the waves" was to be challenged by the Spanish Armada and the pope's desire to conquer the British Isles.

While the Armada carried a superior fighting force and perhaps could have attained the pope's objective of usurping English influence and the Jesuit objective of stopping Protestantism, a powerful storm prevailed and much of the Armada sank without ever firing a shot. The portion of the Armada that survived that great storm of 1588 was engaged by the British navy, and the Armada was turned back.

Neither the papacy nor the Jesuits were to prevail over England, and British soil became fertile ground for the Protestant Reformation.

It was to be a mere 23 years between the

sinking of Rome's hope with the Armada and the printing of the King James Bible in England. Relying upon the text purchased by the blood of the martyrs, while comparing it with critical text and translations in other languages, the King James Bible was to emerge as God's perfectly preserved words in the English language, standing in opposition to the corrupted critical text of Rome.

The battle between Roman Catholicism and Protestantism was not obfuscated by political correctness or ecumenicism at the time of Luther and the Jesuits: neither was there any doubt that the Bible of Protestantism was dramatically different and often at odds with the Roman Catholic text.

Interestingly, while the critical text of the Catholic church had fourteen additional books, it also had more than two hundred fewer mentions of God the Father, Son and Spirit. One text included verses that the other did not; and no one who was intellectually honest would suggest the two texts were the same, any more than any objective observer would think that Bible-believing Christianity and Roman Catholicism were the same. There might be debate over which was correct, but there would be no debate about their being different.

Consider, from an historical perspective what had taken place in less than one century: In 1517, Luther had posted his ninety-five theses; and in 1611, God's perfectly preserved words were published in the trade language of the world at a time when the English language was inarguably at its quintessential best.

Between 1517 and 1611, Luther published his German Bible (from which we get "Easter" in Acts 12:4) in 1534, the same year that the Church of England broke totally away from the Roman Catholic church. Copernicus argued that the Earth orbited the sun in 1543, and Shakespeare wrote "Hamlet" in 1600. It was a most remarkable century. England had rejected and rebuffed Roman Catholicism, produced the Bible that would become the most influential book ever published in all human history, and put that book on boats that circled the globe: a most amazing turn of events.

The stage was set; and while it took less than one century to accomplish, were it not for the martyr's faithfulness during the previous thousand years, Luther would not have had that text to read. We tend to admire those notable people who advanced Bible-believing Christianity from Luther's day to ours, but we do well to be equally thankful to those maimed yet unnamed, murdered yet unknown martyrs to Roman Catholicism's tyranny.

As the seventeenth century began, there was a surge of exploration, expansion and optimism. Secular Humanistic revisers of history in our politically correct day like to say this happened because "the church" was no longer in control. The truth is that the explorers and scientists of the seventeenth century were church people, just not Roman Catholic church people. The church that no longer exercised control was the paganized, superstitious, murderous church of Rome.

The fresh breath of freedom that began to blow with John Wycliffe had become a history-changing hurricane with Martin Luther, and there was no stopping it.

The catalyst for all this was the rediscovery and recovery of God's words, the Bible of the martyrs that had been protected from Romanism. It was at this time that the centerpiece of activity focused on the words of the Lord, as the Dark Ages and the Inquisition had finally come to their end.

Popes, priests and nuns depicted here supervising a book and Bible burning.

This page from the Wycliffe Bible, decorated at the border and written in the best calligraphy, survived the Dark Ages but most were burned right along with the people who wrote them and read them.

English language Bible translations before 1611

JOHN WYCLIFFE translation of the Bible, published before the time of the Protestant Reformation (in the year 1380), earned Wycliffe the title of "Morning Star of the Reformation." Wycliffe said "The Scriptures are the property of the people, and one which no one should be allowed to wrest from them." Followers of Wycliffe, the Lollards, used the Wycliffe Bible to teach the common man God's words which so angered the Papacy that the Council of Constance ordered all copies of the Wycliffe Bible burned and further, that John Wycliffe's bones be exhumed from the grave and burned. The ashes were thrown into the River Swift, but God's words were more swift and could no longer be bound.

GUTENBERG Bible, printed August 15, 1456, was the wrong text but the advance in technology would allow Bibles to become readily available to increasingly large numbers of people.

WILLIAM TYNDALE translation was published in 1525, eight years after Luther's "Ninety-Five Theses" and eight years before Luther's German Bible. Tyndale was adept in seven languages and resources for his translation Included Jerome's Latin, Greek Hebrew and Aramaic texts and Wycliffe's Bible. Perhaps the second most famous statement made by Tyndale abut his work was written to a Christian leader: "If God spare my lyfe, ere many yeares, I wyl cause a boye that dryveth the plough whall know more o the scripture than thou doest." For his trouble, Tyndale was kidnapped May 21, 1535 and he was strangled and burned at the stake October 6, 1536. It was from that fire that Tyndale made his most famous statement: "Lord, open the King Of England's eyes."

MYLES COVERDALE translation of 1535 with the folio edition being the first complete Bible printed in England. Coverdale's Bible was reprinted in 1550 and 1553 and he went to Geneva to help with the Geneva translation and to England to help with the Great Bible.

THOMAS MATTHEW'S translation was not produced by anyone named Thomas Matthews but by John Rogers, in about 1537. Rogers was concerned about being persecuted for having translated a Bible so he used a pseudonym, but Queen Mary had him burned at the stake nonetheless. The Matthew's Bible contained William Tyndale's previously unpublished translations of Joshua through Second Chronicles.

English language Bible translations before 1611

THE GREAT BIBLE translation was so named because it was produced as a very large book and because King Henry VIII said it was great in that it contained no notes or interpretations. On November 1, 1538, King Henry decreed that every parish set up a Bible "Of the largest volume in English," and so the Great Bible gained a level of prominence beyond that of those previously published.

RICHARD TAVENER translation, published in 1539, was little more than a rewording of the Matthew's Bible text.

BED BUG Bible, published in 1551 by Nicholas Hill, so called because translation of Psalm 91:5 read "so that thou shalt not nede to be afraid of any Bugges by nights."

GENEVA Bible was produced in 1560 and marked the first time an English language Bible was divided into chapters and verses, following the arrangement first used by Robert Eatienne in this fourth edition of the Greek New Testament in 1551. Geneva was also the first to italicize words supplied by the translators. The notes added to the Geneva Bible were markedly Calvinistic, making the Geneva Bible popular with Presbyterians and Baptists even to this present time.

BREECHES Bible, also published in Geneva in 1560, so called because Genesis 3:7 had Adam and Eve sew themselves breeches.

BISHOP'S Bible was published in 1568 as a beautifully illustrated folio, with the work overseen by Matthew Parker. The text most closely resembled that of the Great Bible and that was purposeful as the Bishop's Bible was intended to replace the Great.

KING JAMES Bible was the work of fifty-four scholars and was not known as the "King James" at the time since the King did not translate even one word of the text. Some historians say the King James is little more than a Bishop's Bible while others say it is Tyndale's work. The truth is the translators studied all the contemporary English translations, with the majority and critical Greek Text, and even the Roman Catholic Rheims-Douai that had just been published in 1582 and republished in 1610. There was also careful review of the French, Spanish and Italian texts.

THE "HE" BIBLE was the King James published by Robert Baker with a typographical error changing "she" to "he" in Ruth 3:17.

THE "WICKED" BIBLE was a King James printed in 1631 with the word "not" omitted (probably on purpose by a "printer's devil") from the seventh commandment, so that Exodus 20:14 read "Thou shalt commit adultery."

It should be noted here that the King James translators lacked nothing; and more recent manuscript discoveries duplicate what the King James translators already had, albeit in a different format. Most of the Dead Sea Scrolls were not even Bible, and what little Bible they contained was already known to the King James translators.

Similarly, as the King James translators already had the Roman Catholic translations, they had the same material as subsequently found in Vaticanus and Sinaiticus. The so-called Septuagint was also known to the King James translators although no manuscripts are older than third century A.D., probably making the Septuagint the work of Origen.

The King James translators were divided into six companies, two at Cambridge, two at Oxford and two at Westminster, and each company had specific responsibility to translate specific portions of scripture. Then, as each company would complete its portion, that company would send its work to the other companies for review. Differences of opinion were settled with prayer and debate at group meetings.

Bishop Richard Bancroft gave the charge to the translators to give them a starting point for their work, reproduced for you on the next page.

After four years of work, with the translators' numbers having decreased to forty-seven, two men were chosen from each of the six companies to review the entire work. After thirty-three months, the review was completed and the King James Bible was published in 1611.

It took thirty-three years after the printing had been authorized by the king for the then named "Authorized Version" to become more popular than the Geneva and the Bishop's translations. From 1644, when the final edition of the Geneva Bible was published, the King James was to become the most influential book ever published: God's perfectly preserved words.

Bishop Bancroft's charge to the King James translators

The ordinary Bible read in the Church, commonly called the Bishop's Bible, to be followed, and as little altered as the Truth of the original will permit.

The Names of the Prophets, and the Holy Writers, with the other names of the Text, to be retained, as nigh as may be, accordingly as they were vulgarly used.

The old Ecclesiastical Words to be kept, viz. the Word Church not to be translated Congregation, etc.

When a word hath divers Significations, that to be kept which hash' been most commonly used by the most of the Ancient Fathers, being agreeable to the Propriety of the Place and Analogy of the Faith.

The Division of the Chapters to be altered, either not at all, or as little as may be, if Necessity so require.

No Marginal Notes at all to be affixed, but only for the Explanation of the Hebrew or Greek Words, which cannot without some circumlocution, so briefly and fitly be expressed in the Text.

Such Quotations of Places to be marginally set down as shall serve for the fit Reference of one Scripture to another.

Every particular Man of each Company, to take the same Chapter or Chapters, and having translated or amended them severally by himself, where he thinketh good, all to meet together, confer what they have done, and agree for their Parts what shall stand.

As any one Company hath dispatched any one Book in this Manner they shall send it to the rest, to be considered of seriously and judiciously, for His Majesty is very careful in the Point.

If any Company, upon the Review of the Book so sent, doubt or differ upon any Place, to send them Word thereof; note the Place, and withal send the Reasons, to which if they Consent not, the Difference to be compounded at the General Meeting, which is to be of the chief Persons of each Company, at the end of the Work.

When any Place of special Obscurity is doubted of Letters to be directed, by Authority, to send to any Learned Man in the Land, for his Judgement of such a Place.

Letters to be sent from every Bishop to the rest of his Clergy, admonishing them of this Translation in hand; and to move and charge as many as being skillful in the Tongues; and having taken Pains in that kind, to send his particular Observations to the Company, either at Westminster, Cambridge or Oxford.

The Directors in each Company, to be the Deans of Westminster and Chester for that Place, and the King's Professors in the Hebrew or Greek in either University.

These translations to be used when they agree better with the Text than the Bishop's Bible: Tindoll's, Matthews, Coverdale's, Whitchurche's, Geneva.

Besides the said Directors before mentioned, three or four of the most Ancient and Grave Divines, in either of the Universities, not employed in Translating, to be assigned by the Vice-Chancellor, upon Conference with the rest of the Heads, to be Overseers of the Translations as well Hebrew as Greek, for the better observation of the 4th rule above specified.

There is a myth oft-repeated that the King James of 1611 has been revised five times and that the New King James of the Nelson Publishing Company is merely revision number six. Historically inaccurate, the perpetuation of this myth is really an attempt to undermine belief in the King James as God's perfectly preserved words.

While the publishing company's monetary motivation is easily discerned, why so many others repeat the myth is similarly transparent: they do not believe any Bible ever printed is perfect. If you doubt that, ask them.

The myth of the five revisions is particularly sly in that there is an element of truth to it: there were five editions of the King James Bible and there are differences among them. The myth of the five revisions is intended to give the idea that the text of the King James Bible differs in each of the revisions; and that is simply not true. The myth of the five revisions is intended to make the King James Bible seem as ordinary as any other translation; and that is patently false. Here is what actually happened after the King James Bible was completed in 1611:

The five "revisions" of the King James Bible from 1611 to 1769	
1613 edition	Removed the Apocrypha and repaired typographical errors.
1644 edition	Added a preface by Dr. John Canne which subsequently was removed.
1676 edition	Contained a parallel text by Dr. Scattergood which subsequently was removed.
1680 edition	Added Bishop Ussher's chronology, still available as a study help in some Bibles.
1769 edition	Modernized spelling/orthography (murder for murther) and calligraphy (v is now u).

It is the 1769 edition which we now read. While we know what you mean when you refer to the 1611, you might want to consider using

"1769." When the King James opposition hears you say "1611," they assume you must be an ignorant person, which is what they wanted to believe in the first place. When you say "1769," you are telling King James opponents that you know the score, you know of the five so-called revisions, and you know the Bible text was not changed.

When Nelson Publishing trotted out its New King James, it used the myth of the five revisions in an attempt to validate the text of the "New King Jimmy" which omits the word "Lord" 66 times, "God" 51 times, "heaven" 50 times and omits the words "Jehovah," "damnation" and "devils" entirely.

Here is a verse as you will find it in a King James Bible 1769 edition and the same verse from the page of an actual 1611:

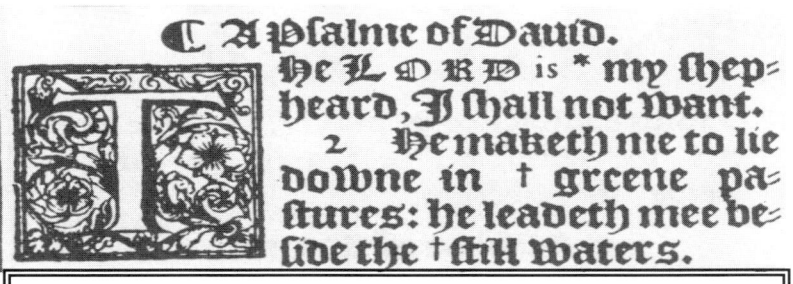

¶ A Psalme of David.
The LORD is * my shepheard, I shall not want.
2 He maketh me to lie downe in † greene pastures: he leadeth mee beside the † still waters.

Psalms 23:1-2 The LORD is my shepherd; I shall not want. He maketh me to lie down in green pastures: he leadeth me beside the still waters.

When you were in grade school your teachers told you about the "long 's'" sound and that is what you see as the first letter on the word "shepheard" in the 1611; so not only is the word spelled differently today, but the letters are shaped differently. Those are changes in orthography and calligraphy, not changes in the text of God's perfectly preserved words in your King James Authorized 1769 Bible.

It is a good thing for you to "know your stuff,"

so here is some additional stuff: The so-called five revisions made more than 30,000 changes but did not change the text! Spelling changes: yes. You see the 1611 example shown spells "shepherd" as "shepheard," "down" as "downe," "green" as "greene," and "me" as "mee." That's four changes in two verses, but not one word of the actual text was changed. See how the 1611 has the "long s" which looks like our letter "f" beginning the words "shepheard" and "shall"? Two more changes in two verses, but the text was not changed.

Another intellectually dishonest tale told by those in opposition to the King James Bible being God's perfectly preserved words is that King James was a homosexual. Since the king did not translate even one word of the Bible that has borne his name, the issue is raised only to elicit sympathy for other translations. While there is no proof, Moody Press and the Moody Broadcasting Network continue to perpetuate this myth, perhaps because Moody is very much invested in the New American Standard translation of the critical text. We would do well to remember that it is God's words that matter, not the men nor their character. After all, Acts 1:16 says that the Holy Ghost spoke by the mouth of a murdering fornicator named King David.

Don't be fooled. Erwin Nestle had not yet been born, but the King James translators had his critical text. The King James translators had the Latin text of the Jesuits, and so they did not need the Siniatic manuscript Count Tichendorf would find nearly two hundred years later. They had the Rheims-Douay of the Roman Catholic church; so they did not have to wait for Bruce Metzgar and Kurt Aland and their United Bible Society text. The King James translators had everything available to them that would be used by translators today, contrary to the misinformation you may have heard.

Don't be fooled. The Dead Sea Scrolls, found in Quamron in 1947, contained very little in the way of Bible text and were mostly secular writings and even a store's inventory list. What Bible they did contain included small portions of Isaiah and Jeremiah which match the Hebrew Masoretic text of the King James Bible and not the Biblica Hebraica of the critical text of the new versions.

Don't be fooled. The Bible produced in 1611 followed a spate of English language Bibles translated at the start of the Reformation and was the capstone: God's perfectly preserved words in the trade language of the world when that language was at its very best.

More people have heard the gospel and been saved through the reading, teaching and preaching of the King James Bible than from the original manuscripts or any other translation.

After 1611, England led the way in exploration and colonization of the world, and those explorers and colonizers carried King James Bibles with them around the globe. This confluence of events led to Bible-based constitutions and governments, such as in the United States of America, to replace repressive Romanism.

When newspaperman Charles Stanley searched Africa to find "Dr. Livingston, I presume," neither your history books at your government school nor the movies told you that Dr. Livingston was a missionary.

For the longest time, during the Dark Ages, the great explorers were Roman Catholics such as Ponce de Leon or Christopher Columbus or Juan Pizzaro. The result of Roman Catholic exploration was never a Republic nor a free and prosperous populace. Roman Catholicism's loss of influence opened the way for people free to read their King James Bibles.

The United States was founded upon Biblical principles, and "separation of church and state" was not an issue then and is not in the Constitution now. The first amendment forbade the nation's being run by any church; but nowhere in the First Amendment was there even the slightest suggestion that the nation should run without any church influence.

When you migrated to America, if you were a Baptist you might seek out other Baptists and gravitate toward Pennsylvania where many had settled. If you were a Congregationalist you might well head for New England.

Back in those days, Roman Catholicism was not welcome and the paganism of the papists was rejected, particularly by the Puritans who even went so far as to ban celebrating the Masse of the Christ (Christmas). One of the colonies did permit the pagan festivities such as tree decorating, gift giving and revelry, and that was the land of the Roman Catholic Mary: Maryland.

Today, it is almost impossible to tell the Protestants from the Catholics and it is fair to say that not only do the Protestants not know what the Catholic church really teaches and vise versa, worst still, neither Protestants nor Catholics even know the doctrines of their own church. Such was not the case in 1611. Today, it is almost impossible to tell the Protestant Bible from the Catholic text; but such was not the case in 1611.

The King James Bible had emerged from among the several English language Bibles produced; and with the benefit of hindsight, there can be no doubt that God's words were working effectually. I Thessalonians 2:13.

From the time of Luther until the dawn of the Machine Age was a time of unparalleled exploration and governmental experimentation. Our form of government was then referred to as the Great Experiment, and the King James Bible was the most influential book on the planet.

The devil had not dozed off, however, but without the power of the pope to advance his nefarious agenda, Satan used his wiles once again to deceive the unsaved and the unwary believers.

By the time the King James Bible had been around two hundred years and was moving into its third century of prominence, there were calls for its revision. Words were said to be archaic and syntax was said to be convoluted and clumsy; but what was really afoot was a plot to move from the majority text of the martyrs to the corrupt critical text of the Catholics.

While no one was suggesting that Shakespeare's plays be rewritten because they contained archaic or difficult words, no such respect was accorded the Bible.

The devil may have whispered in your ear that there are confusing and archaic words in your King James Bible such as, in II Thessalonians 2:7: "only he who now letteth will let." That word "let" means, "to hinder," and you are confused because someone asked you "Who let the dogs out?" and in their question "let" meant to allow, the opposite of hinder.

While it is true that the context helps with getting the definition right, there is also this marvelous invention called the dictionary. Context and dictionary aside, when you watch a tennis match and a serve skims the top of the net, it is called a "let ball" because its progress had been hindered.

King James Bible Statistics

3,586,489 letters

788,258 words

31,102 verses. 1.189 chapters, 66 books

Vocabulary of 12,764 words employed
(Typical adult vocabulary 30,000 words, 500,000 in typical dictionary)

We need not abandon the text of the martyrs for the critical text when there are ways to learn the right material and have God's perfectly preserved words rather than devilish imitation. People who are intellectually lazy are most easily deceived; and those who do not know there are and have always been two streams of Bible manuscripts and translations are especially vulnerable. Not only is not knowing no excuse, not knowing makes it all the easier for Satan to advance his agenda, which, since Genesis chapter three, has been to get people to question God's words.

And so, a committee was formed in the middle of the nineteenth century to evaluate the King James Bible with the goal being to update it to more modern language: very much the same thing we have all heard each time a new translation is published. The hidden agenda was to replace the majority text of the martyrs with the critical text of the infidels.

Two men on the committee were members of the Church of England and each enjoyed the reputation of being a leading scholar of the day. F. J. A. Hort and B. F. Westcott already had produced a Greek translation of the critical text that had come down through time from Origen and Eusebius through the Dark Ages and the papacy into the nineteenth century. Their text came to be known as the Westcott-Hort (W+H) text and was to become the basis of every translation since 1881.

Westcott and Hort were Roman Catholic sympathizers who believed that Protestantism was a temporary aberration which soon enough would pass. The W+H Greek text was to become the focus of the committee involved in updating the King James Bible; but they did not update it, rather they supplanted it.

Brilliant men to be sure, scholarly and erudite, Westcott and Hort and the Greek text that was the product of their collaboration intimidated the committee. "Yea, hath God said?" had advanced from Genesis three to 1881 and persists to this day to all who are not King James Bible believers.

The belief system of Westcott and Hort included:
Racism: blacks were barely human, if human at all
The Occult, including conversations with the dead
Darwinian evolution
Roman Catholicism and Communism, which led them to pray for the destruction of the United States
British Israelism: that America and England are the true Israel.
Denial of the deity of the Lord Jesus Christ

While a few men saw the deception that was taking place and complained at the time, those men were forced to resign from the committee, and so their possible influence was lost. Dean Burgon was most notable among them; and he wrote books against the Westcott-Hort Greek and the resultant English translation until Burgon's great voice and considerable mind were silenced by the grave.

Brilliant scholars, Westcott and Hort worked with a committee of very capable men; but the problem was that their brilliance was invested in the wrong text, the corrupted text of the infidels and the popes. It is as if there is an apostolic succession to intelligent yet unbelieving error that can be traced back to Adamantius Origen, down through Eusebius and Constantine, the Dark Ages with its popes, the Jesuit order, Jermome's Latin Vulgate and the Douay-Rheims.

But up until 1881, the separate streams of manuscripts each flowed through a different bed; and nobody would confuse one with the other. That changed with the confluence of Westcott and Hort and the translations which followed.

This is a most critical point: the corrupted text was being positioned by Westcott and Hort to replace the pure text of the martyrs; and when that was accomplished, every translation produced since 1881 would be based upon the corrupt text rather than the pure.

The translating committee of 1881 replaced the Greek text of the King James Bible with the corrupt text, and the English translation that was published in 1881 was not an updated King James Bible at all. In fact, the 1881 English Revised version of Westcott and Hort, was to become the American Revised Version of 1901; and they are the parents and grandparents of every English translation since, all based upon the corrupt text that had been rejected by the martyrs for centuries.

The Westcott-Hort translation was never about updating the very few archaic words in the King James Bible, it was never about altering punctuation to a more modern style: the W+H translation was all about replacing the Greek text of the King James with the Greek text of the popes.

Fewer than four percent of the Greek manuscripts ever discovered agree with the W+H Greek text while more than ninety-six percent agree with the Majority Text which underlies the King James.

The minority manuscripts were given precedence because of the theory which states that the oldest manuscripts would be superior to all others in that they dated back closer to the time of the writing. Problems with that theory are easily discerned when you remember there were corrupt translations in the first century (II Corinthians 2:17: For we are not as many, which corrupt the word of God:); and it just makes common sense that the paper work of the murderous church run by infidels would survive centuries of time more readily than the paper work of the murdered martyrs.

The misinformation most everyone now believes is that all Bibles are pretty much alike as they are all translated by well-meaning people who all used the same underlying manuscripts. Nothing could be further from the truth.

Not well-meaning at all, the scholars for the most part were unsaved religionists with agendas of personal aggrandizement. Not the same text at all, but texts divergent in more than thirty thousand places, texts related to entirely different belief systems: Bible-believing Christians versus liberal, unbelieving, unsaved social engineers.

The fewer than four percent of the manuscripts were even written in the different Greek dialect of the priest class rather than the koine Greek of the common man, a fact borne witness to by Nestle in his critical apparatus.

The most significant of the fewer than four percent of the texts are named Vaticanus (as it was found in the papal library) and Siniaticus (as it was found in a trash heap at the Roman Catholic monastery near Mount Sinai). Additionally, both Vaticanus and Siniaticus were written on velum made from rolled and cured antelope hide, not from the people's papyrus.

While Vaticanus and Siniaticus may well be the most ancient New Testament Greek scriptures ever found, they are from the fourth century, which means they had plenty of time to have been corrupted. It is most likely that these manuscripts are from the fifty corrupt New Testaments produced by Eusebeus for Constantine. Clearly, it does not follow that they are the best merely because they are the oldest.

We have no originals, after all.

When Count von Tischendorf discovered Siniaticus, he wrote in his journal that his heart beat in his chest as he awaited dawn, at which time he could begin translating the books of the Apocrypha, as he found them in Siniaticus.

Every Bible translated from 1881 on, relying of the fewer than four percent of the manuscripts which include Vaticanus and Siniaticus, should contain all the apocryphal books because those books are in those texts. Imagine how well modern translations would sell to Protestants had they contained the fourteen books of the Roman Catholic apocrypha. Had they been included, everyone would know what you are learning here: every translation since 1881 is a Roman Catholic wolf dressed in Evangelical sheep's clothing.

Forget the so-called ecumenical movement: forget the objective of the Jesuits as they endeavored to stop the spread of Protestantism at all cost: the job had been done. With what Westcott and Hort had accomplished, the Protestant was to believe the best Bible was in the pope's library. Every accredited seminary in America teaches its students that the corrupt Greek text of the murderous Roman Catholic church is the best text and even wrongly refers to it as "the originals."

Satan has deceived the scholars and most of Christianity just as certainly as he tricked Eve into questioning God's words.

The result of the devilish deception was that

the Greek text of the King James Bible, the text which Westcott and Hort literally hated, was replaced by the text traceable back to Origen's Hexapala.

Opposition leader Dean Burgon wrote <u>The Revision Revised</u> to document the deception which had taken place, carefully calling attention to the fact that the oldest manuscripts venerated by Westcott and Hort were Roman Catholic, written in the wrong dialect, written on the wrong sort of material, found in the wrong church.

Were you to take on the task of updating the King James Bible today, you might start by getting every Greek manuscript ever found into your office, and that would be a pile of about five thousand seven hundred, give or take a few.

Upon review of the manuscripts, you might note than more than ninety-six percent of the manuscripts are in substantive agreement with one another and fewer than four percent contrast from that vast majority.

You might also notice that the minority manuscripts have hundreds fewer mentions of the names of deity and thousands fewer words, yet they have the fourteen additional books of the apocrypha.

Next you might assemble translations in other languages to see the translating work which had gone on before. When you add foreign language translations and the English translations which had gone before to your two piles of Greek manuscripts, it would be clear that Roman Catholic texts agree with the fewer than four percent of the manuscripts and the Protestant and Reformation and the text of the martyrs agree with the ninety-six percent majority.

Westcott and Hort, however, advanced the devil's agenda by replacing the King James Greek text with the minority text of the critics. Vaticanus and Siniaticus became the mainstays of Bible translation from that day to this.

Truth available in the King James Bible and no other

Genesis 1:1: In the beginning God created the heaven and the earth. Every new translation says "heavens" plural, which is not true in that God created the two additional heavens when He separated the firmaments.

Matthew 1:25: And knew her not till she had brought forth her firstborn son: and he called his name JESUS. That Jesus was the firstborn of Mary and that Mary had other children is lost in the new translation which are based upon the Roman Catholic mss. which could well make those translations agree with the Catholic error of Mary's having been a perpetual virgin.

II Timothy 2:15: Study to shew thyself approved unto God, a workman that needeth not to be ashamed, rightly dividing the word of truth. Only the King James Bible instructs the believer to study while all the new translations make the issue one of good works.

Galatians 2:7: But contrariwise, when they saw that the gospel of the uncircumcision was committed unto me, as the gospel of the circumcision was unto Peter; Only the King James Bible shows that two gospels were in operation from Acts 9 until Israel's fall.

II Corinthians 2:17: For we are not as many, which corrupt the word of God: but as of sincerity, but as of God, in the sight of God speak we in Christ. Only the King James Bible warns against corrupted Bibles. The new translations warn against selling Bibles.

II Samuel 21:19: And there was again a battle in Gob with the Philistines, where Elhanan the son of Jaareoregim, a Bethlehemite, slew the brother of Goliath the Gittite, the staff of whose spear was like a weaver's beam. Only the King James Bible has Elhanan killing Lahmi, the brother of Goliath, while the newer translations have Elhanan killing Goliath, when we all know David did that.

Ephesians 1:7: In whom we have redemption through his blood, the forgiveness of sins, according to the riches of his grace;
Colossians 1:14 In whom we have redemption through his blood, even the forgiveness of sins:
Only the King James Bible has the blood of Christ in these verses.

Luke 23:33: And when they were come to the place, which is called Calvary, there they crucified him, and the malefactors, one on the right hand, and the other on the left. While hymnals and sermons typically have references to Calvary, that word appears only in the King James Bible.

Isaiah 14:12: How art thou fallen from heaven, O Lucifer, son of the morning! how art thou cut down to the ground, which didst weaken the nations! Lucifer, the name for Satan when he was the covering cherub, appears only in the King James Bible.

Psalms 12:6-7: The words of the LORD are pure words: as silver tried in a furnace of earth, purified seven times. Thou shalt keep them, O LORD, thou shalt preserve them from this generation for ever. Only the King James Bible includes this promise from God to preserve his words.

Two men who lived more than a century ago switched one Greek text for another, and now the vast majority of Evangelicals and Protestants are reading an English translation of the Roman Catholic text.

Any Bible translation produced since 1881 is based upon the minority text, also called the critical text, the text of Roman Catholicism, the text of Origen, Eusebius and Constantine. The Westcott-Hort committee that was supposed to update the King James Bible did not, but brought out the English Revised Bible of 1881 and misled the public into thinking all they had done was to update the King James.

The agreement was that the 1881 was to stand alone for twenty years; so it was not until 1901 that the American Revised Bible was published in the United States, bringing the Westcott-Hort text to churches and bookstores here.

NIV, NASV, Living, Holman, New English, Amplified...every one.

RSV, NRSV, New King James, Message...every one.

TEV, CEV, Tweedle DD...every one.

Go back a hundred years: Darby, Williams, Weymouth, Williams...every one.

If your Bible is not a King James Bible, then your translation has as its final authority that same minority text that was in the hands of the murderous priests of the Dark Ages. As far as what you are reading is concerned, the martyrs died in vain.

You may have believed the devil's sly lie, as it appears in preface of the NIV, which lie is that your modern translation is eclectic, meaning that all texts were considered. Considering all texts and rejecting all texts at points in which they disagree with Westcott-Hort's Vaticanus and Siniaticus would mean, in practice, that only readings in agreement with Westcott-Hort Vaticanus and Siniaticus would pass.

If you had 5600+ marbles in your bath tub and compared them all but you only accepted the fewer than four percent of the marbles which were rosary beads, you could honestly say you had been eclectic and you had compared all the marbles. At the same time you would have told a sly lie and been intellectually dishonest. Start your "eclectic" Bible translation by comparing the 5600+ manuscripts but only use those that match the readings in Vaticanus Siniaticus Westcott-Hort and you've got what has actually happened.

With the notable exception of the King James Bible, every translation sold today has a heritage of heresy traceable all the way back to Genesis three, II Corinthians 2:17, Origen, Eusebius, Constantine, the popes and today's unsaved liberal theologian.

To prove this premise, in the back of this book are charts which list for you those omissions of entire verses and omissions of the names of deity as first omitted in Westcott-Hort and subsequently in Nestles text, United Bible Society text and then omitted in modern translations.

From the charts you see that the issue is not the "thees and thous" or the "milch kines" or "he who letteth will let." Evaluate the quality of the omissions in the critical text and you begin to see the intensity of Satan's attack against our Lord Jesus Christ.

The Nazarene denomination missed it when their leader, Dr. Ralph Earle, became associated with the New International Version translation. While Earle was not a translator, his position on an oversight committee made the N.I.V. attractive to the Nazarene Denomination out of respect for Dr. Earle.

The Nazarenes subsequently signed an agreement whereby that denomination would use only the N.V. in its Sunday School curriculum quarterlies; and in exchange the denomination would get its Sunday School curriculum free from the publisher of the N.I.V.

When Nazarene Evangelist Harold Froge found out from me that the N.I.V. had serious problems, Froge was interested. When I told him that the N.V. did not contain the word "sanctification," that dear old preacher of "second-blessing sanctification" was livid.

No doubt there were other factors as well; but the Nazarene denomination tried to get out of its contract, but could not. The compromise they did reach kept the N.I.V. in their quarterlies; however the King James version was printed right along side. Time passed, Dr. Earle and Evangelist Froge have both passed on, and the old guard of their denomination has been replaced by the new generation that could not care less about the Bible version issue.

The truth of the matter is, very few people care and the devil has the modern church-goer just as wrong as was Eve in the Garden when Satan first encouraged humanity to question and doubt God's words.

It should matter that the Received Text (Textus Receptus) of the King James Bible differs from the Critical Text (Westcott-Hort) in 2,288 places. The more recent Greek text of the United Bible Society (Kurt Aland, Bruce Metzgar, Matthew Black, Allen Wickgren) differs from the Received Text (Textus Receptus) in 2,077 places and from the Nestle Text (23rd) in 2,122 places.

Of the differences between the Received Text and the Critical Texts, the three Critical texts called to your attention here have 2,018 of the variants (97.2%) in common.

That means that new translations which come into the English language from the critical texts will always differ from the King James and almost always differ in the same places.

And the differences matter.

When the word "Lord" is removed from what the dying thief cried from the cross, it matters. (Luke 23:42)

When Saul does not call Jesus Christ "Lord" on the road to Damascus, it matters. (Acts 9:5)

When becoming no more a servant but an heir is not "through Christ," it matters. (Galatians 4:7)

When forgiveness is not "by His blood," it

matters. (Colossians 1:14, Ephesians 1:7)

"And Jesus answered him, saying, It is written, That man shall not live by bread alone, but by every word of God. (Luke 4:4)

It matters.

It turns out our three vocabularies (oral, written and reading) are insufficient, for we need a fourth: God's perfectly preserved words in our King James Bible.

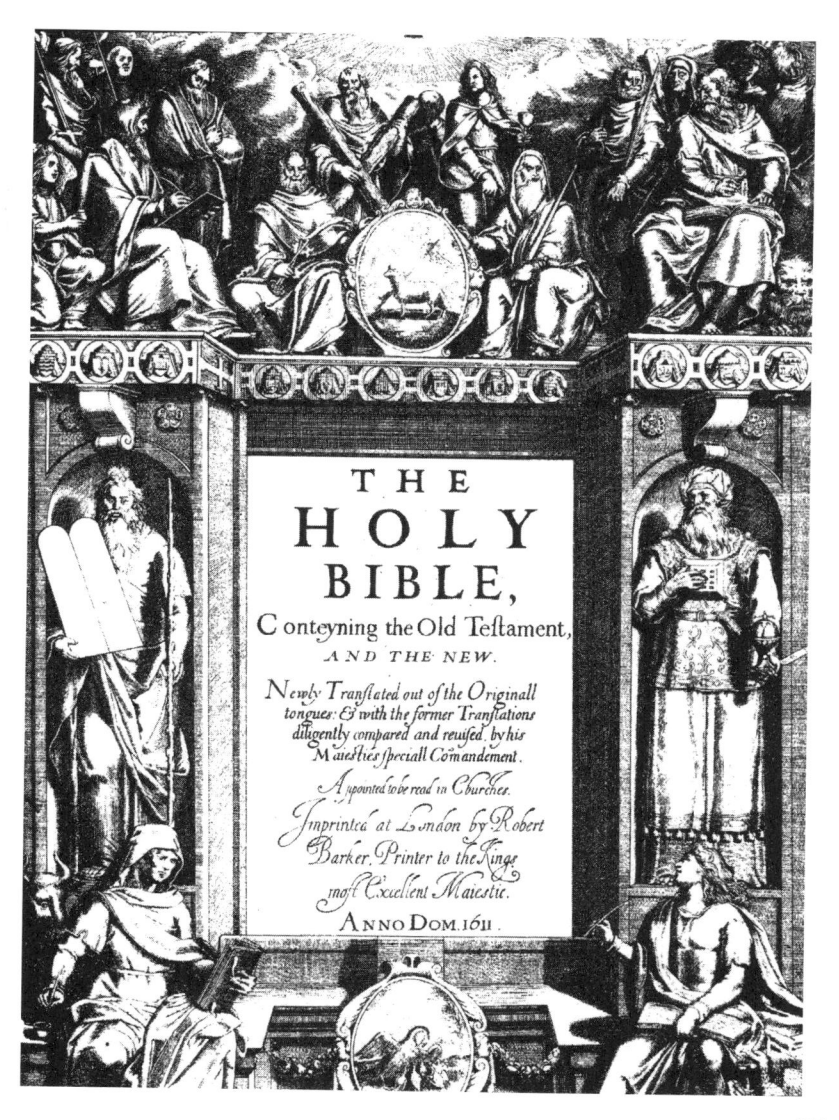

Translator testimonies regarding their work, from infidels:

DR. FRANKLIN LOGSDON, produced the NEW AMERICAN STANDARD for the Lockman Foundation, hired the translators, wrote the preface, spent the last years of his life apologizing for what he had done.

"I must under God renounce every attachment to the New American Standard Version. I'm afraid I'm in trouble with the Lord...we laid the groundwork; I wrote the format; I helped interview some of the translators; I sat with the translators; I wrote the preface...I'm in trouble; I can't refute these arguments; it's wrong, terribly wrong; it's frighteningly wrong; and what am I going to do about it?

When questions began to reach me at first, I was quite offended...I used to laugh with others. However, in attempting to answer, I began to sense that something was not right about the New American Standard Version. I can no longer ignore these criticisms I am hearing and I can't refute them. The deletions are absolutely frightening...there are so many. Are we so naïve that we do not suspect Satanic deception in all of this?

Upon investigation, I wrote my dear friend, Mr. Lockman, emplaning that I was forced to renounce all attachments to the NASV. The product is grievous to my heart and helps to complicate matters in these already troublous times. I don't want anything to do with it.

The finest leaders that we have today...haven't gone into it...the use of the new versions of a corrupted Greek text...just as I hadn't gone into it...that's how easily one can be deceived. You can say the Authorized Version (King James) is absolutely correct. How correct? 100% correct! If you must stand against everyone else, stand..."

DR. A.V. HENDERSON

Baptist Bible College
628 East Kearney
Springfield, Missouri 65803
April 4, 1985

Mr. Terrance McLean

Dear Mr. McLean:

Baptist Bible College teaches the Bible to be inspired in its' original writings but we do not teach continued revelation. We use the King James Bible in our classrooms because we consider it a good translation. We recommend the searching for meaning of Bible words through all available sources.

We use the Textus Receptus in Greek classes but we are not into translation too much in undergraduate work.

We appreciate your concern and inquiry.

Sincerely,

A. V. Henderson
President

50 E. Foothill Blvd. · Arcadia, CA 91006 · (818) 445-1579

January 13, 1987

Mr. Terence D. McLean
McLean's Christian Bookstores

Dear Mr. McLean:

Thank you for your most recent correspondence. We are committed to the importance of communication between our listeners and this ministry. Therefore, we appreciated hearing from you again. Dr. Dobson did read both your letters and asked me to express his regards (and the thoughts in this letter).

We regret that you perceived our previous reply as inadequate. We certainly attempt to respond personally to each letter in order to deal with the issues being raised. Unfortunately, the tremendous volume of mail we handle at times will cause haste in our response. Although we were somewhat disturbed by your lack of understanding, we would like to address the specific questions that you raised.

First, Dr. Dobson is a fourth generation member of the Church of the Nazarene. He does not belong to the Church of Christ, nor does he share its entire theology.

Secondly, please understand that Dr. Dobson is not a theologian, nor has he attempted to analyze the entire text of The International Children's Bible. The shortcoming in this translation which you mentioned was a surprise to him. And, if your information is accurate, it would represent a position with which Dr. Dobson disagrees.

However, it is difficult to find a translation that some evangelical group does not find fault with. As for Focus on the Family, we distribute more than a million dollars worth of books and materials each year, and it is impossible for Dr. Dobson to review every word of each publication. Nevertheless, he is blamed whenever an inconsistency is spotted. I'm sure you can understand the difficult position in which this places him, and hope you will pray for him as he seeks to serve the Lord in this heavy responsibility.

Dedicated to the Preservation of the Home • James C. Dobson, Ph.D., President

WORD OF GRACE

November 12, 1985

Terry McLean
Hilltop Acres

Dear Terry,

Thanks so much for writing. We are glad to have your response to our broadcast, and we appreciate this opportunity to correspond on a personal level.

I am including some material that I really hope you will take the time to read. The idea that the KJV is the Word of God as opposed to other translations is simply not true, and cannot be supported either biblically or academically. The Bible was originally written in Hebrew, Aramaic and Greek, and it is only the original writings that were inspired by God. He has certainly had His hand in the transmission of His Word, as verified by the fact that the Bible is by far the most well-preserved book of antiquity. But when a scribe copied the text, he was not inspired. However, the fact is, the number of questionable texts is very small, and none affect any major doctrines.

I realize that in some areas of the country, the KJV is believed to be the only God-inspired translation. But this is an untenable position. What about all of the Christians who lived before 1611? Were they without God's Word? And what about the billions of non-English speaking peoples around the world? Are they also without the true Word of God? The answer is no. Although no translation (English or otherwise) is perfect, if the translators have done their homework, we can rest assured that we have a good translation. Thus, I see nothing wrong with using the New American Standard Bible or any other good translation.

I hope this has been helpful and that you will continue to listen and pray for our ministry here at "Grace to You". May God richly bless you as you labor for Him Who is worthy of our utmost.

Yours in His service,

John MacArthur
Pastor-Teacher

Translator testimonies regarding their work from infidels:	
Dr. Virginia Mallencott, style editor for the NEW INERNATIONAL VERSION	"(Jesus) is our elder brother, the trail-blazer and constant companion for us—-ultimately is among many brothers and sisters in an eternal, equally worthy sibling-hood. First born only In the sense that he was the first to show us that it is possible to live in oneness with the divine source while we are here on this planet...I can no longer worship in a theological context that depicts God as an abusive parent *(referring to Christ's death on the cross)* and Jesus as the obedient, trusting child."

Note the difference in the tenor and the tone as we now look at the testimony of King James Bible Believers. The liberal lesbian (Mallencott) stands in stark contrast to the Russian believer (Panin) below. One twisted the Bible to validate her own self-destructive life style while the other held fast to the form of sound words even as the country in which he lived was turning toward Communism.

Translator testimonies regarding their word for believers:	
Russian author Dr. Ivan Panin from the preface to his NUMERIC STUDY BIBLE of 1914	"...the Bible, like the great God Himself, is not to be approached with chatter and clatter and bustle, a la the modern "introductions," Bible Dictionaries, or Cyclopedias Biblical; but with contrite spirit, bruised heart, and prostrate form; but above all with the shoes off the feet, rather than shod with the boots of modern "criticism" (euphemism for guessage mostly) of patent leather, and high heeled, and—-creaking at that."

DAVID OTIS FULLER, D.D.
605 Deming Street, S.E.
P.O. Box 7096
Grand Rapids, Michigan 49510

WHICH King James BIBLE?
VERSION
SOCIETY, INC.

"Of the 100 Versions of the Bible which is nearest to the original manuscripts?"

July 1, 1983

Mr. Terence D. McLean
McLeans Christian Bookstores

Dear Friend McLean;

    Your letter certainly encouraged me and I want to thank you for it. You are on the right track and with God's help and by God's Grace STAY ON IT.

    Yes I know the pressures are terrific but we KNOW we are right, we KNOW that Almighty God has honored and blessed and used the KJV for the past 370 years AND every great revival has come from the KJV. IF--this Sovereign God has done that for His Book I KNOW He expects you and me to do the same and we will C.H.O.H.W (a polite way of saying "Come Hell Or High Water"

    What makes me angry, yes FURIOUS(Jer.6;10,11a) is the way publishers and scholars are hawking and huckstering and merchandising the Holy Word of a Holy God for $$$$$$$$MILLIONS. You may be SURE God Almighty will NOT let that go by default.

    This whole version controversy can be summarized in one word--SATANIC. And that can be proved from Scripture. JUST AS Satan twisted Simon Peter around his little finger and caused him to rebuke the Lord and our Lord replied in those searing, scorching words "GET THEE BEHIND ME SATAN" JUST SO Satan has a MULTITUDE yes that is the word A MULTITUDE of born again, blood bought Christians to rebuke the Holy Spirit, "Holy Spirit You are in grave error in keeping that verse in Your Bible and You need to correct a serious mistake in a verse that needs to be changed....etc. THAT in my book is next door to the unpardonable sin.

    z"WHEN THE ENEMY COMES IN LIKE A FLOOD, THE SPIRIT OF THE LORD WILL RAISE UP A STANDARD AGAINST HIM" There it is, God's ironclad promise. I believe revival is coming and with it persecution and opposition we have never witnessed before, but it WILL NEVER COME until this multitude of Christians are deeply convicted of this awful sin of kicking God's Word around like a football

    It is downright GOOD to know of your two stores being "KJV only" Keep on keeping on like that in honoring God. God is pleased with just such clearcut action. God has given us a sacred and holy mission to accomplish as long as He gives us breath. He EXPECTS US to let the whole world know that we face as of NOW the most vicious and malicious attempted assassination of the Character, the Name, the Word of God ever done on planet earth since those blasphemous words were uttered in Eden very WORD of God is pure." (Prov. 30:5) "Thou hast magnified thy WORD above all thy Name." (Psalm 138:2b)

"YEA HATH GOD SAID' IF--you or I had a close friend or loved one who was being slandered and vilified, we would spring to their defense and stand by them and with them and for them C.H.O.H.W.(a polite way of saying "Come Hell Or High Water") HOW MUCH MORE should we stand by and for and with this Lovely Son of God Jesus Christ AND His Holy Word found in the KJV, Who has done SO MUCH for us.

    I am enclosing some pamphlets which perhaps you haven't seen This one by Norman Ward is a masterpiece. He is a security guard at GM in Indianapolis and has had NO formal Bible training but he writes like a scholar.

    More and MORE am I seeing and hearing from laymen and some ministers too, who have had their eyes opened and are not afraid to stand up and be counted. r Sure, we will lose friends and make enemies but my reply is "SO WHAT?" "Shall WE be carried to the skies, On flowry beds of ease, While others fought to win the prize, And sailed thru bloody seas."

    After all Terence it doesn't make Any difference what happens to you or to me but it make a GREAT difference what happens to the Cause of Christ and some day soon you and I will stand before a Holy God and give an account as to what we did or did NO:T do to try and wake up sleeping, snoring, smugly contented Christians to the deadly peril we face ; the rug is being pulled from under us with this spate of 100 PERversions AND the wool has been pulled over our eyes for the past 100 years ever since the publication of the Revised Version of 1881 where ALL THIS MISCHIEF BEGAN

    Have you contacted Kregel Publishers here in G.R. for the good discount rzte they give to Bookstores? Zondervan put out one o my first books 40 years ago or more, The Treasury of David, a condensatio of his seven volume set(Charles Haddon Spurgeon) from several millions words down to several hundred thousand; I like Pat. Z. but it makes me angry at the way he pushes this NIV which is one of the worst(read Daniel 3;25b and see)

    One morning at breakfast some weeks ago Pat passed our table and held out a book, the KJV and said,"Doc, You see this book, I use this in devotions and speaking." I said,"That's fine Pat, but let me ask you a question, Do you make that Book your final, absolute Authority, the true, pure, infallible, inerrant Word of God?" He paused a moment and then said, "Yes I do" Then I asked him "Why Pat do you publish and sell the NIV" And he replied "Because it is easier to read!

    WHAT A COPOUT! Who in the world teaches us the Bible, the Holy Spirit of Course. Pat Z. can't get away with that, God won't let him. If God handled Uzzah and Uzziah(II Sam.6 and II Xhron.26) I know He will handle All who MIShandle His Holy Word. Uzzah did what he did with the best of intentions but he was a corpse the moment he touched the ark.

    God bless you Terence. SO glad to hear from you. If you have anything to ask me or confer with me about don't hesitate to call me collect (616) GL 2-4204

    Keep looking UP! Its MUCH MUCH later than we think! And THAT is the understatement of ALL understatements for the year!

                                              Faithfully yours

Jer.6;10,11a
Isa. 8;19,20
READ! KJV

Translator testimonies regarding their work from believers:

From the "Translators to the Reader: as found in the KING JAMES BIBLE

"The originall thereof being from heaven, not from earth; the authour being God, not man: the editer, the holy spirit, not the wit of the Apostles or Prophets; the Pen-men such as were sanctified from the wombe, and endewed with a principall portion of Gods spirit; the matter, veritie, pietie, puritie, uprightnesse; the forme, Gods word, Gods testimonie, Gods oracles, the word of trueth, the word of salvation, & the effect, light of understanding, stablenesse of perswasion, repentance from dead workes, newnesse of life, holinesse, peace, ioy in the holy Ghost; lastly, the end and reward of the studie thereof, fellowship with the Saints, participation of the heavenly nature, fruition of an inheritance immortall, undefiled, and that never shall fade away: Happie is the man that delighteth in the Scripture, and thrise happie that meditateth in it day and night.

King James the First personally authored hymns, sermons and gospel tracts; but he did not translate so much as one word of the Bible that bears his name. On July 22, 1604, the king announced he had appointed 54 scholars to produce a new Bible translation without notes favoring any theological slant.

The John Rylands Fragment shown here is one of the more than 5,600 manuscript evidences for the New Testament, this from the Gospel of John. There are more than 13,000 manuscript evidences when you include other writings such as hymnals, sermon books and journals.

Entire verses listed are in the King James Bible and the majority Greek text (Textus Receptus) but are omitted or called into question with brackets in other Greek texts or modern English translations, as shown in the table below. All English language translations since 1881 have most of these problems.

Verses listed are in the KJV	Westcott-Hort text of 1881	Nestle's 23rd text of 1957	United Bible Society text of 1976	New American Standard 1971	Revised Standard 1953	NIV translation 1973
Mt. 12:47	Omitted	Bracketed	Bracketed		Omitted	
17:21	Omitted	Omitted	Omitted	Omitted	Omitted	Omitted
18:11	Omitted	Omitted	Omitted	Bracketed	Omitted	Omitted
21:44	Bracketed	Bracketed	Bracketed		Omitted	
23:14	Omitted	Omitted	Omitted	Bracketed	Omitted	Omitted
Mk. 7:16	Omitted	Omitted	Omitted	Omitted	Omitted	Omitted
9:44	Omitted	Omitted	Omitted	Omitted	Omitted	Omitted
9:46	Omitted	Omitted	Omitted	Omitted	Omitted	Omitted
11:26	Omitted	Omitted	Omitted	Omitted	Omitted	Omitted
15:28	Omitted	Omitted	Omitted	Omitted	Omitted	Omitted
16:9-20	Bracketed	Bracketed	Bracketed	Bracketed	Omitted	
Lk. 17:36	Omitted	Omitted	Omitted	Omitted	Omitted	Omitted
22:20	Bracketed	Bracketed				
22:43	Bracketed	Bracketed	Bracketed			
22:44	Bracketed	Bracketed	Bracketed		Omitted	
23:17	Omitted	Omitted	Omitted	Omitted	Omitted	Omitted
24:12	Bracketed	Omitted		Bracketed	Omitted	
24:40	Bracketed	Omitted		Omitted	Omitted	
John 5:4	Omitted	Omitted	Omitted	Omitted	Omitted	Omitted
7:53-8:11	Bracketed	Omitted	Bracketed		Omitted	
Acts 8:37	Omitted	Omitted	Omitted	Omitted	Omitted	Omitted
15:34	Omitted	Omitted	Omitted	Omitted	Omitted	Omitted
24:7	Omitted	Omitted	Omitted	Omitted	Omitted	Omitted
28:28	Omitted	Omitted	Omitted	Omitted	Omitted	Omitted
Ro. 16:24	Omitted	Omitted	Omitted	Omitted	Omitted	Omitted
I John 5:7	Omitted	Omitted	Omitted	Omitted	Omitted	Omitted
Totals	18 verses	31 verses	17 verses	16 verses	46 verses	17 verses

Names of Deity, present in the King James Bible and the Majority Text, absent from the critical Greek texts and translations produced since 1881 (such at the NASV, RSV and NIV).						
Names of deity which are in KJV	Westcott Hort 1881	Nestle 23rd 1957	United Bible Society 1976	New American Std. 1973	Revised Standard 1953	NIV translation 1973
Matthew 4:12 Jesus	Omitted	Omitted	Omitted	Omitted	Omitted	
4:18 Jesus	Omitted	Omitted	Omitted	Omitted	Omitted	
4:23 Jesus	Omitted	Omitted	Omitted		Omitted	
6:33 Jesus	Omitted	Omitted	Bracketed	Omitted	Omitted	Omitted
8:3 Jesus	Omitted	Omitted	Omitted	Omitted	Omitted	
8:5 Jesus	Omitted	Omitted	Omitted	Omitted	Omitted	
8:7 Jesus	Omitted	Omitted	Omitted	Omitted	Omitted	
8:29 Jesus	Omitted	Omitted	Omitted	Omitted	Omitted	Omitted
9:12 Jesus	Omitted	Omitted	Omitted	Omitted	Omitted	
12:15 Jesus	Omitted	Omitted	Omitted	Omitted	Omitted	
13:36 Jesus	Omitted	Omitted	Omitted	Omitted	Omitted	Omitted
13:51 Jesus	Omitted	Omitted	Omitted	Omitted	Omitted	
13:51 Lord	Omitted	Omitted	Omitted	Omitted	Omitted	Omitted
14:14 Jesus	Omitted	Omitted	Omitted	Omitted	Omitted	
14:22 Jesus	Omitted	Omitted	Omitted	Omitted	Omitted	
14:25 Jesus	Omitted	Omitted	Omitted	Omitted	Omitted	
15:16 Jesus	Omitted	Omitted	Omitted	Omitted	Omitted	
15:30 Jesus	Omitted	Omitted	Omitted	Omitted	Omitted	Omitted
16:20 Jesus	Omitted	Omitted	Omitted	Omitted	Omitted	Omitted
17:11 Jesus	Omitted	Omitted	Omitted	Omitted	Omitted	Omitted
17:20 Jesus	Omitted	Omitted	Omitted	Omitted	Omitted	Omitted
18:2 Jesus	Omitted	Omitted	Omitted	Omitted	Omitted	Omitted
18:11 Son	Omitted	Omitted	Omitted		Omitted	Omitted
19:17 God	Omitted	Omitted	Omitted	Omitted	Omitted	Omitted
21:12 God	Omitted	Omitted	Omitted	Omitted	Omitted	Omitted
22:30 God	Omitted	Omitted	Omitted	Omitted	Omitted	Omitted
22:32 God	Omitted	Omitted	Omitted		Omitted	Omitted
22:37 Jesus	Omitted	Omitted	Omitted	Omitted	Omitted	
23:8 Christ	Omitted	Omitted	Omitted	Omitted	Omitted	Omitted

Names of deity which are in KJV	Westcott Hort 1881	Nestle 23rd 1957	United Bible Society 1976	New American Std. 1973	Revised Standard 1953	NIV translation 1973
Matthew 24:2 Jesus	Omitted	Omitted	Omitted	Omitted	Omitted	Omitted
25:13 Son	Omitted	Omitted	Omitted	Omitted	Omitted	Omitted
28:6 Lord	Omitted	Omitted	Omitted	Omitted	Omitted	Omitted
Mk. 1:1 God	Omitted	Omitted	Omitted			
1:41 Jesus	Omitted	Omitted	Omitted	Omitted	Omitted	
5:13 Jesus	Omitted	Omitted	Omitted	Omitted	Omitted	Omitted
5:19 Jesus	Omitted	Omitted	Omitted	Omitted	Omitted	
6:34 Jesus	Omitted	Omitted	Omitted	Omitted	Omitted	Omitted
7:27 Jesus	Omitted	Omitted	Omitted	Omitted	Omitted	Omitted
8:1 Jesus	Omitted	Omitted	Omitted	Omitted	Omitted	
8:17 Jesus	Omitted	Omitted	Omitted		Omitted	
9:24 Lord	Omitted	Omitted	Omitted	Omitted	Omitted	Omitted
10:6 God	Omitted	Omitted	Omitted		Omitted	
10:52 Jesus	Omitted	Omitted	Omitted	Omitted	Omitted	
11:10 Lord	Omitted	Omitted	Omitted	Omitted	Omitted	Omitted
11:11 Jesus	Omitted	Omitted	Omitted	Omitted	Omitted	
11:14 Jesus	Omitted	Omitted	Omitted	Omitted	Omitted	Omitted
11:15 Jesus	Omitted	Omitted	Omitted	Omitted	Omitted	
11:26 Father	Omitted	Omitted	Omitted	Omitted	Omitted	Omitted
12:27 God	Omitted	Omitted	Omitted	Omitted	Omitted	Omitted
12:32 God	Omitted	Omitted	Omitted	Omitted	Omitted	
12:41 Jesus	Omitted	Omitted	Omitted	Omitted	Omitted	
14:22 Jesus	Omitted	Omitted	Omitted	Omitted	Omitted	
14:45 Master	Omitted	Omitted	Omitted	Omitted	Omitted	Omitted
Luke 2:40 Spirit	Omitted	Omitted	Omitted	Omitted	Omitted	Omitted
4:4 God	Omitted	Omitted	Omitted	Omitted	Omitted	Omitted
4:41 Christ	Omitted	Omitted	Omitted	Omitted	Omitted	Omitted
7:22 Jesus	Omitted	Omitted	Omitted	Omitted	Omitted	Omitted
7:31 Lord	Omitted	Omitted	Omitted	Omitted	Omitted	Omitted

Names of Deity, present in the King James Bible and the Majority Text, absent from the critical Greek texts and translations produced since 1881 (such at the NASV, RSV and NIV).

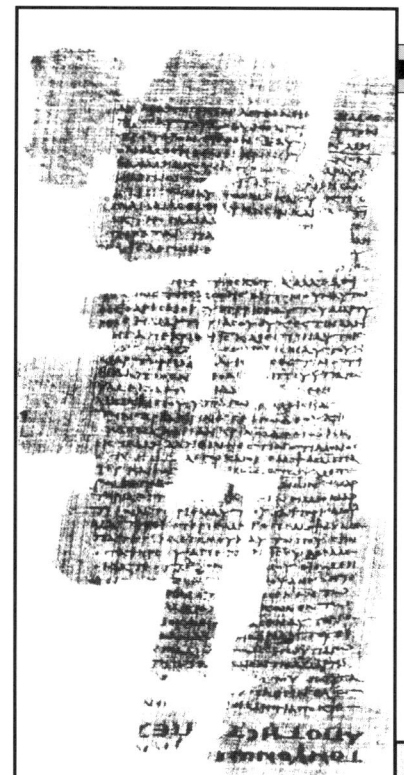

Shown at left is the Bodmer Papyrus, which lacks John 7:53 through John 8:11, that being why most translations since 1881 put those verses in brackets or have a note calling the authenticity of those verses into question. However, all mss. agree that John 8:12 should read: "Then spake Jesus again", which is only true when you include Christ speaking the first time, which means John 7:53-8:11 belongs in the text; for without them, John 8:12 would be Christ's speaking the first time.

Shown at right is the Chester Beatty papyrus P46 showing I Corinthians 1:24 through 2:2. This manuscript is the source of the debate as to whether the Bible should refer to the "mystery" or to the "testimony" of Christ, clearly a textual issue with a doctrinal agenda.

Names of Deity, present in the King James Bible and the Majority Text, absent from the critical Greek texts and translations produced since 1881 (such at the NASV, RSV and NIV).						
Names of deity which are in KJV	Westcott Hort 1881	Nestle 23rd 1957	United Bible Society 1976	New American Std. 1973	Revised Standard 1953	NIV translation 1973
Luke 8:38 Jesus	Omitted	Omitted	Omitted	Omitted	Omitted	
9:43 Jesus	Omitted	Omitted	Omitted	Omitted	Omitted	
9:57 Lord	Omitted	Omitted	Omitted	Omitted	Omitted	Omitted
9:59 Lord	Omitted	Omitted	Omitted	Omitted		Omitted
9:60 Jesus	Omitted	Omitted	Omitted	Omitted	Omitted	
10:21 Jesus	Omitted	Omitted	Omitted	Omitted	Omitted	
12:31 God	Omitted	Omitted	Omitted	Omitted	Omitted	Omitted
13:2 Jesus	Omitted	Omitted	Omitted	Omitted	Omitted	
13:25 Lord	Omitted	Omitted	Omitted	Omitted	Omitted	Omitted
21:4 God	Omitted	Omitted	Omitted	Omitted	Omitted	Omitted
22:31 Lord	Omitted	Omitted	Omitted	Omitted	Omitted	Omitted
22:63 Jesus	Omitted	Omitted	Omitted			
23:42 Lord	Omitted	Omitted	Omitted	Omitted	Omitted	Omitted
23:43 Jesus	Omitted	Omitted	Omitted	Omitted	Omitted	
24:36 Jesus	Omitted	Omitted	Omitted	Omitted		
John 3:2 Jesus	Omitted	Omitted	Omitted	Omitted		
3:34 God	Omitted	Omitted	Omitted	Omitted	Omitted	
4:16 Jesus	Omitted	Omitted	Omitted	Omitted		Omitted
4:42 Christ	Omitted	Omitted	Omitted	Omitted	Omitted	Omitted
4:46 Jesus	Omitted	Omitted	Omitted	Omitted	Omitted	Omitted
5:17 Jesus	Omitted	Omitted	Bracketed	Omitted		
5:30 Father	Omitted	Omitted	Omitted	Omitted	Omitted	Omitted
6:14 Jesus	Omitted	Omitted	Omitted	Omitted	Omitted	
6:39 Father's	Omitted	Omitted	Omitted	Omitted	Omitted	Omitted
6:69 Christ	Omitted	Omitted	Omitted	Omitted	Omitted	Omitted
8:1 Jesus	Bracketed	Omitted	Bracketed		Omitted	
8:4 Master	Bracketed	Omitted	Bracketed		Omitted	
8:6 Jesus	Bracketed	Omitted	Bracketed		Omitted	
8:9 Jesus	Omitted	Omitted	Omitted	Omitted	Omitted	

Names of Deity, present in the King James Bible and the Majority Text, absent from the critical Greek texts and translations produced since 1881 (such at the NASV, RSV and NIV).

Names of deity which are in KJV	Westcott Hort 1881	Nestle 23rd 1957	United Bible Society 1976	New American Std. 1973	Revised Standard 1953	NIV translation 1973
John 8:10 Jesus	Bracketed	Omitted	Bracketed		Omitted	
8:11 Lord	Bracketed	Omitted	Bracketed		Omitted	Omitted
8:11 Jesus	Bracketed	Omitted	Bracketed		Omitted	
8:16 Father	Bracketed	Omitted		Omitted	Omitted	
8:20 Jesus	Omitted	Omitted	Omitted	Omitted	Omitted	Omitted
8:21 Jesus	Omitted	Omitted	Omitted	Omitted	Omitted	
8:29 Father	Omitted	Omitted	Omitted	Omitted	Omitted	Omitted
9:35 God	Omitted	Omitted	Omitted	Omitted	Omitted	Omitted
11:45 Jesus	Omitted	Omitted	Omitted	Omitted	Omitted	
13:8 Jesus	Omitted	Omitted	Omitted			
13:32 God	Omitted		Bracketed			
16:16 Father	Omitted	Omitted	Omitted	Omitted	Omitted	Omitted
18:5 Jesus	Omitted	Omitted	Omitted	Omitted		
19:38 Jesus	Omitted	Omitted	Omitted	Omitted	Omitted	Omitted
18:39 Jesus	Omitted	Omitted	Omitted	Omitted	Omitted	Omitted
Acts 2:30 Christ	Omitted	Omitted	Omitted	Omitted	Omitted	Omitted
3:36 Jesus	Omitted	Omitted	Omitted	Omitted	Omitted	Omitted
4:24 God	Omitted	Omitted	Omitted	Omitted	Omitted	Omitted
7:30 Lord	Omitted	Omitted	Omitted	Omitted	Omitted	Omitted
7:32 God	Omitted	Omitted	Omitted	Omitted	Omitted	Omitted
7:32 God	Omitted	Omitted	Omitted	Omitted	Omitted	Omitted
7:37 Lord	Omitted	Omitted	Omitted	Omitted	Omitted	Omitted
7:46 God		Omitted	Omitted		Omitted	Omitted
8:37 Jesus	Omitted	Omitted	Omitted	Omitted	Omitted	Omitted
8:37 Christ	Omitted	Omitted	Omitted	Omitted	Omitted	Omitted
8:37 God	Omitted	Omitted	Omitted	Omitted	Omitted	Omitted
9:5 Lord	Omitted	Omitted	Omitted	Omitted	Omitted	Omitted
9:6 Lord	Omitted	Omitted	Omitted	Omitted	Omitted	Omitted
9:6 Lord	Omitted	Omitted	Omitted	Omitted	Omitted	Omitted

Names of Deity, present in the King James Bible and the Majority Text, absent from the critical Greek texts and translations produced since 1881 (such at the NASV, RSV and NIV).

Names of deity which are in KJV	Westcott Hort 1881	Nestle 23rd 1957	United Bible Society 1976	New American Std. 1973	Revised Standard 1953	NIV translation 1973
Acts 9:29 Jesus	Omitted	Omitted	Omitted	Omitted	Omitted	Omitted
15:11 Christ	Omitted	Omitted	Omitted	Omitted	Omitted	Omitted
15:18 God	Omitted	Omitted	Omitted	Omitted	Omitted	Omitted
16:31 Christ	Omitted	Omitted	Omitted	Omitted	Omitted	Omitted
19:4 Christ	Omitted	Omitted	Omitted	Omitted	Omitted	Omitted
19:10 Jesus	Omitted	Omitted	Omitted	Omitted	Omitted	Omitted
20:21 Christ	Omitted	Omitted	Omitted			Omitted
22:16 Lord	Omitted	Omitted	Omitted	Omitted	Omitted	Omitted
23:9 God	Omitted	Omitted	Omitted	Omitted	Omitted	Omitted
Ro. 1:16 Christ	Omitted	Omitted	Omitted	Omitted	Omitted	Omitted
6:11 Lord	Omitted	Omitted	Omitted	Omitted	Omitted	Omitted
8:1 Spirit	Omitted	Omitted	Omitted	Omitted	Omitted	Omitted
14:6 Lord	Omitted	Omitted	Omitted	Omitted	Omitted	Omitted
15:8 Jesus	Omitted	Omitted	Omitted	Omitted	Omitted	Omitted
15:19 God	Omitted	Omitted	Bracketed	Omitted	Omitted	Omitted
16:18 Jesus	Omitted	Omitted	Omitted	Omitted	Omitted	Omitted
16:20 Christ	Omitted	Omitted	Omitted	Omitted		Omitted
16:24 Lord	Omitted	Omitted	Omitted	Omitted	Omitted	Omitted
16:24 Jesus	Omitted	Omitted	Omitted	Omitted	Omitted	Omitted
16:24 Christ	Omitted	Omitted	Omitted	Omitted	Omitted	Omitted
I Cor 1:14 God	Omitted	Omitted	Bracketed		Omitted	Omitted
5:4 Christ	Omitted	Omitted	Omitted	Omitted	Omitted	Omitted
5:5 Jesus	Omitted	Omitted	Omitted			Omitted
6:20 God's	Omitted	Omitted	Omitted	Omitted	Omitted	Omitted
9:1 Christ	Omitted	Omitted	Omitted	Omitted	Omitted	Omitted
9:18 Christ	Omitted	Omitted	Omitted	Omitted	Omitted	Omitted
10:28 Lord's	Omitted	Omitted	Omitted	Omitted	Omitted	Omitted
11:29 Lord's	Omitted	Omitted	Omitted	Omitted	Omitted	
15:47 Lord	Omitted	Omitted	Omitted	Omitted	Omitted	Omitted

Names of deity which are in KJV	Westcott Hort 1881	Nestle 23rd 1957	United Bible Society 1976	New American Std. 1973	Revised Standard 1953	NIV translation 1973
I Cor. 16:22 Jesus	Omitted	Omitted	Omitted	Omitted	Omitted	Omitted
16:22 Christ	Omitted	Omitted	Omitted	Omitted	Omitted	Omitted
16:23 Christ	Omitted	Omitted	Omitted	Omitted	Omitted	Omitted
II Cor. 4:6 Jesus	Omitted	Omitted	Bracketed	Omitted	Omitted	Omitted
4:10 Lord	Omitted	Omitted	Omitted	Omitted	Omitted	Omitted
5:18 Jesus	Omitted	Omitted	Omitted	Omitted	Omitted	Omitted
10:7 Christ's	Omitted	Omitted	Omitted	Omitted	Omitted	Omitted
11:31 Christ	Omitted	Omitted	Omitted	Omitted	Omitted	Omitted
Gal. 1:5 God	Bracketed	Omitted	Bracketed	Omitted	Omitted	
3:17 Christ	Omitted	Omitted	Omitted	Omitted	Omitted	Omitted
4:7 Christ	Omitted	Omitted	Omitted	Omitted	Omitted	Omitted
6:15 Christ	Omitted	Omitted	Omitted	Omitted	Omitted	Omitted
6:15 Jesus	Omitted	Omitted	Omitted	Omitted	Omitted	Omitted
6:17 Lord	Omitted	Omitted	Omitted	Omitted	Omitted	Omitted
Ep. 3:9 Jesus	Omitted	Omitted	Omitted	Omitted	Omitted	Omitted
3:9 Christ	Omitted	Omitted	Omitted	Omitted	Omitted	Omitted
3:14 Lord	Omitted	Omitted	Omitted	Omitted	Omitted	Omitted
3:14 Jesus	Omitted	Omitted	Omitted	Omitted	Omitted	Omitted
3:14 Christ	Omitted	Omitted	Omitted	Omitted	Omitted	Omitted
5:9 Spirit	Omitted	Omitted	Omitted	Omitted	Omitted	Omitted
Ph. 4:13 Christ	Omitted	Omitted	Omitted	Omitted	Omitted	Omitted
Col. 1:2 Lord	Omitted	Omitted	Omitted	Omitted	Omitted	Omitted
1:2 Jesus	Omitted	Omitted	Omitted	Omitted	Omitted	Omitted
1:2 Christ	Omitted	Omitted	Omitted	Omitted	Omitted	Omitted
1:28 Jesus	Omitted	Omitted	Omitted	Omitted	Omitted	Omitted
2:2 Father	Omitted	Omitted	Omitted	Omitted	Omitted	Omitted
I Th. 1:1 God	Omitted	Omitted	Omitted	Omitted	Omitted	Omitted
1:1 Father	Omitted	Omitted	Omitted	Omitted	Omitted	Omitted
1:1 Lord	Omitted	Omitted	Omitted	Omitted	Omitted	Omitted

Names of deity which are in KJV	Westcott Hort 1881	Nestle 23rd 1957	United Bible Society 1976	New American Std. 1973	Revised Standard 1953	NIV translation 1973
I Th. 1:1 Jesus	Omitted	Omitted	Omitted	Omitted	Omitted	Omitted
1:1 Christ	Omitted	Omitted	Omitted	Omitted	Omitted	Omitted
2:19 Christ	Omitted	Omitted	Omitted	Omitted	Omitted	
3:11 Christ	Omitted	Omitted	Omitted	Omitted	Omitted	Omitted
3:13 Christ	Omitted	Omitted	Omitted	Omitted	Omitted	Omitted
II Th. 1:8 Christ	Omitted	Omitted	Omitted	Omitted	Omitted	Omitted
1:12 Christ	Omitted	Omitted	Omitted	Omitted	Omitted	Omitted
2:4 God	Omitted	Omitted	Omitted	Omitted	Omitted	Omitted
I Tim. 1:1 Lord	Omitted	Omitted	Omitted	Omitted	Omitted	Omitted
2:7 Christ	Omitted	Omitted	Omitted	Omitted	Omitted	Omitted
3:16 God	Omitted	Omitted	Omitted	Omitted	Omitted	Omitted
5:21 Lord	Omitted	Omitted	Omitted	Omitted	Omitted	Omitted
Ti. 1:4 Lord	Omitted	Omitted	Omitted	Omitted	Omitted	Omitted
Ph. Vs. 6 Jesus	Omitted	Omitted	Omitted	Omitted	Omitted	Omitted
He. 3:1 Christ	Omitted	Omitted	Omitted	Omitted	Omitted	Omitted
10:9 God	Omitted	Omitted	Omitted	Omitted	Omitted	Omitted
10:30 Christ	Omitted	Omitted	Omitted	Omitted	Omitted	Omitted
Ja. 1:12 Lord	Omitted	Omitted	Omitted		Omitted	Omitted
I Pe. 1:22 Spirit	Omitted	Omitted	Omitted	Omitted	Omitted	Omitted
5:10 Jesus	Omitted	Omitted	Omitted	Omitted	Omitted	Omitted
5:14 Jesus	Omitted	Omitted	Omitted	Omitted	Omitted	Omitted
I Jn. 1:7 Christ	Omitted	Omitted	Omitted	Omitted	Omitted	Omitted
3:16 God	Omitted	Omitted	Omitted	Omitted	Omitted	Omitted
4:3 Christ	Omitted	Omitted	Omitted	Omitted	Omitted	Omitted
5:7 Father	Omitted	Omitted	Omitted	Omitted	Omitted	Omitted
5:7 Word	Omitted	Omitted	Omitted	Omitted	Omitted	Omitted
5:7 Holy Ghost	Omitted	Omitted	Omitted	Omitted	Omitted	Omitted
5:13 Son	Omitted	Omitted	Omitted	Omitted	Omitted	Omitted
5:13 God	Omitted	Omitted	Omitted	Omitted	Omitted	Omitted

Names of Deity, present in the King James Bible and the Majority Text, absent from the critical Greek texts and translations produced since 1881 (such at the NASV, RSV and NIV).

Names of Deity, present in the King James Bible and the Majority Text, absent from the critical Greek texts and translations produced since 1881 (such at the NASV, RSV and NIV).

Names of deity which are in KJV	Westcott Hort 1881	Nestle 23rd 1957	United Bible Society 1976	New American Std. 1973	Revised Standard 1953	NIV translation 1973
II John 3 Lord	Omitted	Omitted	Omitted	Omitted	Omitted	Omitted
Vs. 9 Christ	Omitted	Omitted	Omitted	Omitted	Omitted	Omitted
Jude 4 God	Omitted	Omitted	Omitted	Omitted	Omitted	Omitted
Revelation 1:8 Beginning	Omitted	Omitted	Omitted	Omitted	Omitted	Omitted
1:8 Ending	Omitted	Omitted	Omitted	Omitted	Omitted	Omitted
1:9 Christ	Omitted	Omitted	Omitted	Omitted	Omitted	Omitted
1:11 Alpha	Omitted	Omitted	Omitted	Omitted	Omitted	Omitted
1:11 Omega	Omitted	Omitted	Omitted	Omitted	Omitted	Omitted
1:11 First	Omitted	Omitted	Omitted	Omitted	Omitted	Omitted
1:11 Last	Omitted	Omitted	Omitted	Omitted	Omitted	Omitted
12:17 Christ	Omitted	Omitted	Omitted	Omitted	Omitted	Omitted
14:5 God	Omitted	Omitted	Omitted	Omitted	Omitted	Omitted
16:5 Lord	Omitted	Omitted	Omitted	Omitted	Omitted	Omitted
19:1 Lord	Omitted	Omitted	Omitted	Omitted	Omitted	Omitted
20:9 God	Omitted	Omitted	Omitted	Omitted	Omitted	Omitted
20:12 God	Omitted	Omitted	Omitted	Omitted	Omitted	Omitted
21:3 God	Omitted	Omitted	Omitted	Omitted	Omitted	
21:4 God	Omitted	Omitted	Omitted	Omitted	Omitted	Omitted
22:12 Christ	Omitted	Omitted	Omitted	Omitted	Omitted	Omitted

Names of Deity, sorted by name, by text, with totals.

Name	W & H	Nestle	UBS	NASV	RSV	NIV
Jesus	78	82	75	73	73	39
Christ	43	44	44	43	42	43
Lord	36	37	35	35	36	35
God	37	38	32	33	24	31
Others	27	29	26	26	28	26
Total	221	230	212	210	203	174

Afterward...

Hi, there.

I am your Bible and you have not looked at me in an awfully long time.

You bought me just about this time last year.

When you brought me home from the store, I so looked forward to having my pages turned and my content read over and over, but the first thing you did was to put me in a fancy zipper case with several colored markers, and I did not see the light of day for weeks after that.

There was one day when you unzipped my vinyl-that-looks-like-leather prison and wrote on my dedication page. That was nice.

It was then that you zipped up the zipper case and put me in a place of particular honor. You placed me on top of a large box that lights up, a mysterious box that you stare at several hours each and every day.

One day it was late, nearly midnight, and I heard from the mysterious box underneath me that a new year was about to begin and the very next day I thought things had really changed. You opened the zipper case and read some of my pages each day of the new year, but that only lasted for about a month.

When you stopped reading you left a piece of

paper that says "Read the Bible Through in a Year" in the book of Numbers.

By February, my case was pretty dusty and I had not been looked at for what seemed like eternity.

When it got to be March, the dust got wiped off and you began to search my pages looking for verses that would help you to win an argument you were having at the office. When you could not find what you were looking for you plopped me down grumbling about having lost something called a "bet." I must have really let your down because you left me on the floor next to the mysterious box, and you did not even stick me back in my vinyl-that-looks-like-leather prison.

Some old people came to visit one time and one of them rescued me from the floor and read my content every day. How nice that was, as my pages were turned with such care and devotion, but when those old people left, that was that.

You went to a wedding in May. I did not get to go, but you brought some of the flowers home and pressed one of them between my pages, which now have some green stains just where Jesus says "Man shall not live by bread alone, but by every word of God."

Unfortunately, the placing of flowers from the wedding started a trend and by June I was starting to feel like a scrapbook. There are now newspaper clippings, ribbons and more flowers between my pages.

It was in July that you went on vacation and decided to take me along on the trip. The suitcase was very uncomfortable, but I didn't mind because I wanted to be there for you whenever you might need me.

After about a week, you took me out of the suitcase and put me in the middle of the kitchen table. There were several people seated in the kitchen which made me very excited because I was just sure we were going to have a Bible study.

Instead of reading my content, however, all you did was look at the flowers and the clippings from the newspaper, and before you could say "Study to shew yourself approved unto God," I was returned to the suitcase.

When we got back home you took me from the suitcase and put me back on top of the mysterious box, which I had learned was called a TV set. My next door neighbor was called the "TV Guide" and you read his content every week and then threw him out and got another one. It was September and apparently something called "sweeps month" was very important to you.

One of the old people that had visited, the one that read my content so intently, got very sick and you actually opened me up and read a Psalm that day. It was exciting for me, but you seemed sad.

The next month I found out that the old person who had read so many of my pages had died and that is when you put me in the middle of the coffee table because your Pastor was coming over to see you.

When I found out that the old person who had died was your parent and that your Pastor was going to talk with you, I had hopes that you would take an interest in me the way that your parent had.

When you handed me to your Pastor and asked him to show you what heaven is like, your Pastor said we couldn't be sure because, after all, we did not have the original manuscripts and no translation is totally accurate.

You seemed a little bit upset. You took me back from your Pastor and opened me to where the wedding flowers had been pressed and you asked your Pastor what Jesus meant when Christ said "Man shall not live by bread alone, but by every word of God."

Your Pastor told you that verse was not in the manuscripts that most scholars relied upon and that many theologians had concluded that Jesus never actually made that statement.

That was when I went back into my vinyl-made-to-look-like-leather prison and this time you stuck me in a bookcase and I have been there ever since. My pages pressing the flowers are now so stained that the words on those pages are illegible, but that doesn't matter anymore, does it?

Terence D. McLean

BIBLIOGRAPHY

As noted at the outset, "History of Your Bible, proving the King James to be God's perfectly preserved words" is a message taught by the author in more than 150 churches and a score of radio stations. One particular church invited Pastor Terence D. McLean to speak on the Bible version issue. McLean and the host pastor were seated next to each other as the choir sang, and McLean asked his host how much time was allotted for the message. The host pastor asked "Will five minutes be enough?" Realizing the host pastor was serious, McLean graciously said "That will be fine." And fine it was as those five minutes were sufficiently spell-binding that the host pastor subsequently had McLean for a Bible Conference for six consecutive days, more than an hour each meeting, and McLean taught both the five minutes and the more than eight hours...without notes. His ability to do that is a product of the books listed below in this Bibliography of Pastor Terence D. McLean's personal library of books dealing with textual criticism. In addition, McLean has more than one hundred fifty translations of the Bible, scores of books dealing with language and etymology and dozens of books and hundreds of audio messages related to the subject of transmission and translation of the Biblical text.

ALEXANDRIAN CULT: Volumes 1 through 8, Dr. Peter S. Ruckman, Bible Baptist Bookstore Press

BELIEVING BIBLE STUDY, Dr. Edward F. Hills, Christian Research Press

BIBLE BABEL, Dr. Peter S. Ruckman, Bible Believer's Press

BIBLE IN ENGLISH, David Daniell, Yale University Press

BIBLE TRANSLATIONS AND HOW TO CHOOSE BETWEEN THEM, Alan S. Duthie, Paternoster House Press

BIBLE VERSION MANUAL, Donald T. Clarke, Bible Truth Institute

BLIND GUIDES, Dr. Gail Riplinger, AV Publications

BOOKS AND THE PARCHMENTS: How we got our English Bible, F. F. Bruce, Fleming H. Revell Company

BREIF HISTORY OF ENGLISH BIBLE TRANSLATIONS, Laurence M. Vance, Vance Publications

CAMBRIDGE HISTORY OF THE BIBLE: From the Beginnings to Jerome, Edited by P. R. Ackroyd and C. F. Evans, Cambridge University Press

CAMBRIDGE HISTORY OF THE BIBLE: the West from the Fathers to the Reformation, Edited by G. W. H. Lampe, Cambridge University Press

CAMBRIDGE HISTORY OF THE BIBLE: the West from the Reformation to the Present Day, Edited by S. L. Greenslade, Cambridge University Press

CHRISTIAN LIAR'S LIBRARY, Dr. Peter S. Ruckman, Bible Baptist Bookstore Press

CHRISTIAN'S HANDBOOK OF BIBLICAL SCHOLARSHIP, Dr. Peter S. Ruckman, Bible Baptist Bookstore Press

CHRISTIAN'S HANDBOOK OF MANUSCRIPT EVIDENCE, Dr. Peter S. Ruckman, Pensacola Bible Press

COMING OF THE KING JAMES GOSPELS, Ward S. Allen, University of Arkansas Press

COUNTERFEIT OR GENUINE: The Last Twelve Verses of Mark, David Otis Fuller, Various Publishers

DEAD SEA SCROLLS, Miller Burrows, Viking Press

DEAD SEA SCROLLS TRANSLATED: The Qumran Texts In English, Florentino Garcia Martinez, Wm. B. Eerdman's Publishing

DOUBLE JEOPARDY: The New American Standard Update, Laurence M. Vance, Vance Publications

EARLIEST GOSPEL MANUSCRIPT? The Qumran Fragment 7Q5 and its Significance for new Testament Studies, Carsen Peter Thiede, The Paternoster Press

EARLY MANUSCRIPTS & MODERN TRANSLATIONS of the New Testament, Philip Wesley Comfort, Baker Books

ERRORS IN THE KING JAMES BIBLE, formerly titled PROBLEM

TEXTS, Dr. Peter S. Ruckman, BB Bookstore Press

EVALUATING VERSIONS OF THE NEW TESTAMENT, Edward W. Fowler, Maranatha Baptist Bible College Press

FAMINE IN THE LAND, Norman Ward, Which Bible Society Press

GOD'S SECRETARIES: the Making of the King James Bible, Adam Nicolson, Harper Collins Publishers

GOD'S WORD FOR TODAY, Ivan L. Burgener, Berean Bible Fellowship

GREEK NEW TESTAMENT, edited by Kurt Aland, Matthew Black, Carlo M Martini, Bruce M. Metzger, United Bible Society Press

GUIDE TO THE TEXTUAL CRITICISM OF THE NEW TESTAMENT, Edward Miller, Dean Burgon Society Press

HERESIES OF WESTCOTT & HORT, Dr. D. A. Waite, Bible For Today Publishing

HISTORICAL CRITICISM OF THE BIBLE: Methodology or Ideology?, Eta Linnemann, Baker Book House

HOLY BIBLE, REVISED STANDARD, Harper Collins Publishing

IDENTITY OF THE NEW TESTAMENT TEXT, Wilbur N.. Pickering, Zondervan Publishing, OP

IF THE FOUNDATIONS BE DESTROYED, Chick Salliby, Word and Prayer Ministries Publications

IN AWE OF THE WORD, Dr. Gail Riplinger, AV Publications

INDESTRUCTABLE BOOK, Ken Connolly, Baker Book House
INSPIRATION AND INTERPRETATION, Dean John William Burgon, Bible For Today Publications

KING JAMES BIBLE, Various publishers

KING JAMES ONLY, James White, Bethany House Publishing

KING JAMES ONLYISM Versus SCHOLARSHIP ONLYISM, Dr. Peter S. Ruckman, Bible Believer's Press

KING JAMES VERSION DEFENDED, Dr. Edward F. Hills, Christian Research Press

KING JAMES VERSION OF THE BIBLE, Dr, Seven Houck, Peace Protestant Reformed Publicaitons

LANGUAGE OF THE KING JAMES BIBLE, Dr. Gail Riplinger, AV Publications

LOGICAL CRITICISMS OF TEXTUAL CRITICISM, Gordon H. Clark, The Trinity Foundation

MAJORITY TEXT: Essays and Reviews in the Continuing Debate, Theodore P. Letis, Institute For Biblical Textual Studies

MAKING OF THE NEW REVISED STANDARD VERSION OF THE BIBLE, Bruce M. Metzger, Robert C. Dentan, Walter Harrelson, Wm. B. Eerdman's Publishing

MAKING OF THE NIV, Kenneth L. Barker, Baker Book House

MEN BEHIND THE KJV, Gustavus S. Paine, Baker Book House

MODERN BIBLE TRANSLATIONS: Unleashed, Russell R. Standish & Colin D. Standish, Hartland Publications

MODERN BIBLES–THE DARK SECRET, Jack A. Moorman, Foundation Press Publications

MYTHOLOGICAL SEPTUAGINT, Dr. Peter S. Ruckman, Bible Believer's Press

NEW AGE BIBLE VERSIONS, Dr. Gail Riplinger, AV Publications

NEW AMERICAN STANDARD BIBLE, Lockman Foundation, various publishers

NEW INTERNATIONAL VERSION, International Bible Society, various publishers

NEW INTERNATIONAL VERSION, G. W. Anderson, D. E. Anderson, Oldham & Manton Ltd.

NEW TESTAMENT: An Introduction to its Literature and History, J. Gresham Machen, Banner of Truth Trust

NEW TESTAMENT IN ORIGINAL GREEK, edited by B. F. Westcott, F. J. A. Hort, Macmillan·Company, Harper Publishing

NEW TESTAMENT from the Greek Text as Established by Bible Numerics, Ivan Panin, Book Society of Canada Press

NEW TESTAMENT OF THE GREEK TEXT (Textus Receptus) Trinitarian Bible Society

NOVUM TESTAMENTUM GRAECE edited by Erwin Nestle, 23rd edition, various publishers

PERFECTED OR PERVERTED, Norman Ward, Which Bible Society Press

QUEST FOR THE ORIGINAL TEXT of the New Testament, Philip Wesley Comfort, Baker Book House

REAL KING JAMES, David Ralston, Tabernacle Baptist Press

REVISION REVISED, Dean John William Burgon, Dean Burgon SocietySovereign Press

SITTING IN JUDGEMENT OF THE WORD OF GOD, Dr. John Adair, BBB Publications

SOLVING THE MYSTERY OF THE DEAD SEA SCROLLS, Edward M. Cook, Zondervan Publishing

SO MANY VERSIONS: 20th Century English Versions of the Bible, Sakae Kubo & Walter F. Specht, Zondervan Publishing

TRANSLATORS REVIVED, Alexander McClure, R. E. Publications

TRUE OR FALSE, David Otis Fuller, Various Publishers

UNHOLY HANDS ON THE BIBLE VOLUME I: A Comparison Between Six Major Bible Versions, Edited by Jay P. Green, Sovereign Grace Trust Fund Publishing

UNHOLY HANDS ON THE BIBLE VOLUME II: An Introduction to Textual Criticism, Edited by Jay P. Green, Sovereign Grace Trust Fund Publishing

WHICH BIBLE, David Otis Fuller, Various Publishers

WHICH TRANSLATION DO YOU PREFER? Carol E. Miller, Rapids Christian Press

WHICH VERSION NOW? Bob Sheehan, Carey Publications

WHY I BELIEVE THE KING JAMES BIBLE IS THE WORD OF GOD, Dr. Peter S. Ruckman, Bible Believer's Press

WORD OF GOD ON TRIAL, Robert J. Barnett, Bible Literature Distribution

WORDS ABOUT THE WORD: A Guide to Choosing and Using Your Bible, John R. Kohlenberger III, Zondervan Publications

"With A Bible In My Hand" weekly newspaper columns were honored with three prestigious Amy Awards for excellence in Christian writing in the secular press. More than 700 editorials written by Terence D. McLean appeared in local, regional and national publications and the contributions of McLean's columns were twice cited by the Ohio State Legislature as "insightful and extraordinary ... positive contributions" Politics, religion, the world, the flesh, and the devil, are the chapter headings under which thirty -three columns appear, including the first of the Amy Award winners. "With A Bible In My Hand" appeared most often on the editorial page because of its content. Written with humor and a light touch, the most important issues of the day were deftly handled "With A Bible In My Hand."

Order one copy for $6 retail
 plus postage of $2.13, total $8.13.
- Order five copies for $30 and we pay (U,S.) postage.
- Ten for $60, fifteen for $90, we pay (U.S.) postage.

Larger orders save one dollar per book:
- Order in multiples of Twenty for $100, (forty for $200, sixty for $300 and so on), we pay (U.S.) postage.

Send your Check or Money Order to:
discerning the times publishing co. inc.
Post Office Box 87
Alpha OH 45301

What does it mean to be Mid Acts Dispensational? What are the basic doctrines that make Bible-believing Mid-Acts Dispensationalism different, distinct, and definitively correct? This book presents the Mid Acts Dispensational position with clarity and precision. Every new convert, every visitor to any Mid Acts group, every person you want to help see the revelation of the mystery needs a copy of this 114 page perfect bound book.

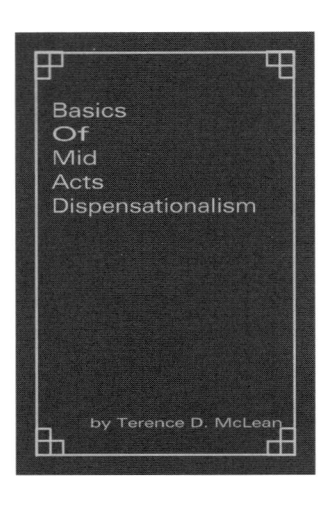

Basics
Of
Mid
Acts
Dispensationalism

by Terence D. McLean

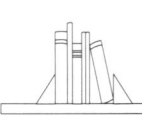

- Order one copy for $5 retail plus actual book rate postage of $1.59, total $6.59

- Order five copies for $25 and we pay postage (in the Continental United States).

- Ten for $50, fifteen for $75, and we pay postage (in the Continental United States).

- Order in multiples of Twenty for $80, (forty for $160, sixty for $240 and so on...)

Send your Check or Money Order to:
discerning the times publishing co. inc.
Post Office Box 87
Alpha OH 45301

How does a person get to heaven? Follow Patty through her neighborhood as she keeps asking her most important question until she gets the right answer. This is an outstanding evangelistic tool. 32 pages of well written and beautifully illustrated material making the gospel of the Grace of God clear and accessible.

- Order one copy for $3 retail plus actual postage of $1.35, total $4.35

- Order five copies for $15 and we pay postage (in the Continental United States).

- Ten for $30, fifteen for $45, and we pay postage (in the Continental Unites States).

- Order in multiples of Twenty for $50, (forty for $100, sixty for $150 and so on)

Send your Check or Money Order to:
discerning the times publishing co. inc.
Post Office Box 87
Alpha OH 45301

The New Life in Jesus Christ is actually a compilation of messages preached by Dr. C.I. Scofield to his congregations at Dallas, Texas and Northfield, Massachusetts. These were published in the "Christian Worker's Magazine" and then published in book form by the Bible Institute Colportage Association in 1915. These messages, subtitled 'Messages of Joy and Victory' are republished now, newly annotated with the benefit of clear dispensational understanding.

- Order one copy for $5 retail plus actual book rate postage of $2.13, total $7.13.
- Order five copies for $25 and we pay postage (in the Continental United States)
- Ten for $50, fifteen for $75, and we pay postage (in the Continental United States).
- Order in multiples of Twenty for $80, (forty for $160, sixty for $240 and so on...)

Send your Check or Money Order to:
discerning the times publishing co. inc.
Post Office Box 87
Alpha OH 45301

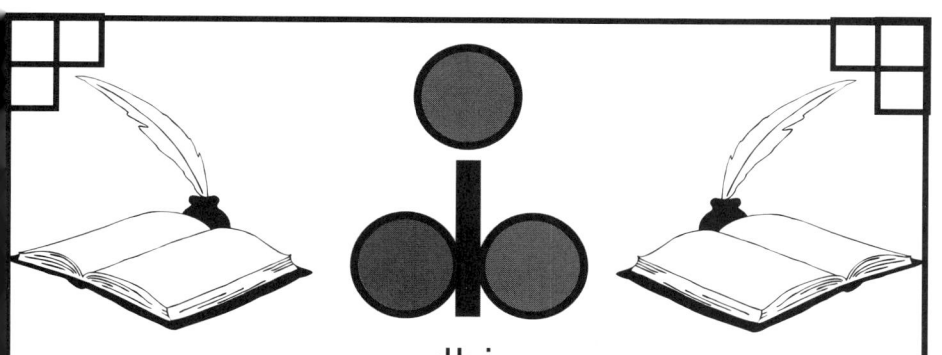

dbi
dispensational
bible
institute
FREE
on the internet:
www.discerningthetimespublishing.com

These video classes are recorded in Windows Media Video (WMV) format and are intended for broadband (DSL, Cable, Satellite) and play on Windows MediaPlayer.

Dial-up Internet access to DBI will not work: for you, Dispensational Bible Institute is available in three other formats.
1. Twenty-nine two hour DVD's to play on your television set, DVD players and computers with DVD players for $200.00
2. Fifteen four hour video CD's to play on your computer using Windows Media Player for $100.00 (They will not play in your car's CD player)
3. Another format for DBI also available is on 2 CD's for $50 with zip files which you can play on your computer using Windows Media Player.

Send your Check or Money Order to:
discerning the times publishing co. inc.
Post Office Box 87
Alpha OH 45301